Understanding Leadership

JOHN FINNEY

Foreword by Bishop George Carey

DATE DUE

daybreak

London

First published in 1989 by
Daybreak
Darton, Longman and Todd Ltd
89 Lillie Road, London SW6 1UD

British Library Cataloguing in Publication Data

Finney, John
   Understanding leadership
   1. Christian life. Leadership
   I. Title
   248.4

ISBN 0–232–51785–1

Quotations from the Bible are mostly taken from
the Authorised Version or the New International Version

Phototypeset by Input Typesetting Ltd,
London SW19 8DR
Printed and bound in Great Britain by
Anchor Press Ltd, Tiptree, Essex

Dedicated to the glory of God
and to all called to be leaders in his church

Contents

Foreword

As a diocesan bishop in the Church of England I can speak with some feeling about the importance of leadership. You show me a growing church, where people are being added to the faith and growing in it, and you will be showing me effective leadership because such things do not simply happen on their own. Churches and fellowships grow because of visionary leadership. Conversely, when churches lose heart and fade away, often, although not always, it is connected with 'leaders' who cannot lead.

I believe that a major challenge facing the Christian church in Britain today is that we must raise up a new breed of leaders – clergy and lay, men and women – who can harness the latent skills of local church life. But often the cry goes up, 'What is the secret of effective leadership? How can the local church develop leadership skills? What makes a Christian leader?'

It is because this is such a crucial area that I have much pleasure in commending John Finney's book. John and I have been friends for many years and I can speak with some knowledge of him and his ministry. He is no 'ivory tower' writer pontificating from on high. Rather he speaks with an authority which comes from first-hand experience and skills developed as an incumbent, diocesan missioner and conference speaker. But it is a further pleasure to write the Foreword to a book which is well researched, well prepared and which is so practical. I have no doubt that this is a book which is a *must* for all churches who want to be more effective.

George Carey
Bishop of Bath and Wells

Preface

In 1966, while browsing through the station bookstall before a train journey, I bought a small book on management theory. I found it fascinating, because the problems it described were the same as those I was facing in my leadership of a smallish village church at that time. In a rather desultory way I kept up my reading of such material, until I took on my present job which requires me to visit and advise many churches. I soon saw that far too many churches had leaders who were uncertain of the skills they needed and where they could find them. A few had swallowed management theory without any thought, while a much greater number had never made use of it and were hostile to the very idea.

The church has always tended to put on the clothes of the latest secular fashion rather belatedly. Having bedecked itself it ventures out only to find it is out of date. Management theory is here to stay, but the church tends to adopt the theories of yesteryear rather than current thinking.

Every survey of churches has shown the importance of leadership. Yet until recently there has been little attempt by Christians to think carefully about the skills and attitudes which leaders require. As a result those in leadership have had to turn to secular management models. These can be helpful, but they have to be used with much care. It has to be recognised that they are built not on any biblical basis but on premises of profit and loss, and may involve manipulation and coercion which are not appropriate or possible in a Christian setting.

But, while this is true, management theory talks mainly about people working together. How do they interact? How do groups cope with change and inertia? How can structures help or hinder the attainment of the goals of an organisation? The church also deals with people. It would be foolish for it to ignore this work and fail to understand its own life better.

This book seeks to lay a firm foundation for a scriptural understanding of leadership and to link it with the most useful material from management theory. Naturally I would insist that before such theory is looked at the biblical view of leadership is established. If management is studied before Scripture there is a danger of adopting secular models, and then reading into Scripture what we want to find.

I also wish to establish that the 'led' are at least as important as the 'leader'. Sometimes books on management give the impression that those who are on the receiving end of leadership are so many potatoes, without individual quirks and visions. If the goal of Christian leadership is to 'present everyone mature in Christ' (Col. 1:28 RSV) then we must constantly be aware of the reactions, feelings, spiritual awareness and personal difficulties of those in the congregation and beyond.

This book would never have been written without the encouragement of my family and their help and forbearance when I disappeared for hours to pound my Amstrad. To have a husband around the house who was 'in, but not available' was not easy and Sheila has been wonderfully accepting of my eccentricities. Felicity Lawson, Director of Ministerial Training in Wakefield, suggested the title and gave much advice, as did other friends and colleagues. The 'Changing Church' course in Birmingham was an enormous stimulus to thought, and it was the exposure to the members of that course which eventually prodded my lethargy into action. However, my deepest thanks must go to those many, many churches and clergy who have invited me to share their life and learn from their experience, not least those in the Diocese of Southwell where I have spent 23 happy years of ministry.

John Finney

Introduction

Imagine two meetings. The agenda is identical, even the membership is the same. Only the chairman is different in each case. One meeting grinds to an exhausted halt after three hours of disputation, while the other reaches its end within the hour with clearcut decisions in a friendly atmosphere.

In any human grouping the importance of the leader can hardly be overemphasised. Whether it be a national government or a gardening club, a factory or the local scouts, the quality of those who are running the organisation is crucial. The only exception is the very small circle of friends who organise, decide and act without any clear leadership; but if even that group grows it will have to change its style of work or perish.

Yet curiously within the church the subject of leadership is treated with some disdain. Every study shows that leadership is pivotal to the growth or decline of a church. Indeed it is almost comical to plot a graph showing the numbers in a church over the years and see how they rose when 'Mr X' was minister and declined under 'Mr Y'. Where statistics have been gathered they have shown conclusively that the character, the spiritual depth, and the leadership qualities of the minister are key factors in the morale, growth and effectiveness of the church.[1] What is true of the minister is also true of other leadership functions within the church – house groups, church socials, evangelistic efforts are all largely dependent upon those who organise them.

But there has been a reluctance to accept this fact. There is a feeling that the church is not as other organisations, and so is governed by different rules: it is a spiritual body under the

Kingship of Christ, not a human structure run by the vicar. Partly this is a defence mechanism to protect the clergy – if the church declines then it is not their fault. Partly it is because the scriptural words about leadership can, at first reading, suggest that it should somehow be different within the church – 'it shall not be so among you'[2] is burnt deep into the memories of all Christians.

The emphasis on what is variously called the 'ministry of all the baptised', 'every-member ministry' or 'freeing the frozen' has rightly shifted the spotlight from the minister to the people. But team ministry of this kind demands accomplished leaders. The 'one-man band' personality cult which dominated the church for so long requires only limited skills from the minister as he organises his 'helpers'. To guide and encourage a team of gifted individuals is much more subtle, complex and demanding.

This change of outlook within the life of the church is only one of a host of other changes. Liturgical renewal, the increasing influence of the diocese,[3] the unscrambling of previously tight theological positions, the ecumenical dimension, spiritual renewal, have all had their effect upon the local congregation. I was ordained into the Church of England in 1958. It was an utterly predictable job. The Prayer Book services were the same as they had always been, the church organisations carried on in the same old way, the clergy–lay relationship was that of pastor and flock. There were rumblings of change in the distance through the Parish and People movement and suchlike which were discussed in a desultory way at clergy gatherings, but they had not yet affected the ordinary parish. The Roman Catholic church down the road sang its Latin Mass, while the Methodists round the corner used Wesley's hymns as they had always done: very few had even heard that there was a Pentecostal church. Thirty years later the Church of England, like every other denomination, has changed and is continuing to change. Often the shifts of emphasis have been so subterranean that people do not notice the extent or importance of what has been happening, until some particular episode makes them realise that the landscape has altered and can never be recovered. The introduction of the Alternative Services Book in 1980 seems to have been such a point of recognition for many members of the Church of England.

In part the changes within the church reflect theological advances which have been moving people's thoughts in new directions. Whether the thinking was new or revived from the past, fresh ideas in ecclesiology, ecumenism, liturgy, and even the nature of theology itself have meant that ultimately the practice of the church was bound to change. This has meant that the church has become much more self-conscious. It is more aware of its own life and of the world around. When boundaries were fuzzy much could be ignored. Clearer definitions bring threat.

But it is not only the church which has been changing. The world is being turned upside down. As Alvin Toffler said, we have experienced 'the death of permanence'. Fundamental changes are taking place in every area of life, not only in the technological field but in the domestic and personal world which was considered inviolate. The traditional home is no longer unquestioned: cohabitation, 'serial marriage', the changed role of women, have each undermined that bastion. At the workplace it is not only scientific innovations which have brought change; the attitude to work, the need to move from job to job in mid-career, the pressures of unemployment, the 'rat race' have produced an atmosphere like the Mad Hatter's tea party. Education and the all-pervasive media have brought new expectations and styles of life. A new morality is emerging which does not distinguish between right and wrong, and which is purely pragmatic – 'if it works it's good'. So in many social groupings immorality seems almost old-fashioned. There is only amorality, and we go back to the world before the Law was given.[4] In many areas of Britain, especially the inner city, a new amalgam of belief has begun to solidify: it has been called 'common' or 'implicit' religion and is far distant from orthodox Christianity.[5]

All these changes have fallen most heavily upon one group of people. 'Within industry no one has been more affected than the supervisor, the man so often "in the middle". Almost without exception, each social and technological trend has made his life more difficult.'[6] As a description of most Christian ministers, 'man in the middle' is hard to better. The pressures upon them have increased and are increasing for the same reasons that they are being experienced by middle management: they have to be the mediators of change, helping an often recalcitrant and uncomprehending group of people to come to terms with the reality of the present and the needs of the future. Whether that group is a church congregation, teachers in a school, or workers on the shop floor is immaterial; the dynamics are the same.

Not least among the many pressures on middle management is the difficulty of telling what the future is likely to be. Prognostications are many and varied, but futurology has had a poor record both inside and outside the church.[7] It is not only the date of the Second Coming which is kept from us, but any indication of what will be. In the early 1950s when a computer filled a fair sized room and cost millions of dollars, a group of market researchers sat down to see how many computers they were likely to sell. They eventually decided that there might be about 1000 computers in the world by the year 2000. As in meteorology, short-term forecasts which extrapolate the present are reasonably accurate but it is unwise to alter one's holiday plans on the basis of long-term predictions. Churches are fairly safe to suggest that the immediate outlook is more of the same, but they are unwise to put much faith in speculations about the distant future. It is not often that God uses an Agabus to predict a famine three years away, and still less common for the Church to take as much notice of a prophecy as did the early Christians with their 'collection for the saints'.[8]

Demands on church leaders intensify. People look to them to lead through a rapidly changing environment but they themselves are often groping. They feel themselves to be adrift, while others look to them to be an anchor. This can cause great stress or great creativity, or both. Stress will show itself in different ways in different ministers. Some amble along doing only what is inescapable. Others feel hard done by, and retreat into a hurt reserve. Others again restrict their ministry to what they know they can do well.

But the situation is far from being all negative. The pressures of change are causing creative innovations to bubble up far more vigorously than for many generations. New thinking and new practice tumble into being. Some of it is shortlived, some is muddleheaded, but some is of the Spirit and has the touch of the finger of God. Leadership in the church may be no sinecure nowadays but neither is it dull. It can be enormously satisfying. What Charles Handy says of the business world is true also of the church: 'management is more fun, more creative, more personal, more political and more intuitive than any textbook'.[9] This book can only plot a few of the lessons we have been learning. No book on leadership must ever be an encyclopaedia which answers all questions. It may suggest a few steps for the dance of the Spirit, but it can never be the dance itself.

Above all, the uncertainties have made many return to the living God. Spiritual renewal illuminates much of the scene. Possibly not since the heyday of the Evangelical and Tractarian movements in Britain and the American revivals in the middle of the last century has God been so near the top of the agenda. Individuals have rediscovered prayer, the gifts of the Spirit, the 'wonder, love and praise' of worship. Churches have found that God does exist and is at work within them and their community. Not all renewal has been sensible or godly, any more than it was in the New Testament church, but it has brought a new hope to millions around the world.[10]

It is, of course, far from uniform. Many churches are in slow decline, unaware of what is happening around them. Others sense a world of danger and are not prepared to venture out: 'the sluggard says, "There is a lion outside" '.[11] John Child wrote the following about industrial companies, but it could be said of many churches: 'Among the features which so often mark the struggling organisation are low motivation and morale, late and inappropriate decisions, conflict and lack of coordination, rising costs and a generally poor response to new opportunities and external change.'[12] Other churches have explored new paths but found that they were only blind alleys. But many have struck a rich vein of truth and found the joy and difficulty of true mission.

However, it cannot be said that the church is giving much help to its ministers and other leaders. Theological colleges teach very little about how to run a church, which is what most of their students will spend most of their career doing. Christian leaders are apparently expected to guide, inspire and teach a church by instinct and natural ability. They are given little further training and little supervision. They work largely on their own. The lack of teaching in this area is felt by many ministers. Many of them, on their own initiative and at their own expense, try to gain this expertise after ordination. The growth of Doctor of Ministry courses in the United States and the proliferation of smaller courses in Britain bear witness to this need.[13]

Are ministers leaders, administrators, managers, professionals?

Many church leaders have never bothered with management studies because they did not see themselves as managers. It is all a matter of definitions. 'Leader' is generally used when the personal qualities are uppermost. 'Manager' suggests organisational skills, while 'administrator' implies someone who carries out rather than creates policy.[14] 'Professional' indicates someone with specialised training and qualifications. But a minister, like anyone else who could be described as 'being in charge', does not fulfil only one role. When preaching in church it may well be as leader, but when taking a wedding it is primarily as a professional. As chairman of the church committee the minister coordinates the work of others and acts as a manager, but when sorting out the flower rota the role is that of an administrator. In many ways this is an argument without foundation. Much of any minister's work is managerial whatever title he or she prefers. The sociologist J. H. Fichter wrote, 'in spite of certain differences, the leadership role in religious groups is roughly synonymous with that of management and administration in non-ecclesiastical organisations'.[15]

I suggest that we would be wise to return to the biblical understanding of leadership. A minister is much more than just the manager of a church or a professional exercising certain skills. The New Testament sees ministry as multi-faceted. It cannot be tied down to one title, such as 'servant' or 'pastor', any more than it can be restricted to 'manager' or 'leader'. However Christian ministry today requires managerial, professional, administrative and leadership skills. It would be foolish to ignore the work which has been done in non-ecclesiastical circles in this field over many years, but at the same time it should never become normative, for the Christian leader should take his orders from Christ and not a book on management.

In this book the word 'leader' will be used to describe the people who are 'in charge'. No word is without overtones and 'leader' has many, not all of them helpful; but it has become the normal term and it would be pernickety to alter it. It should also be noted that when 'leader' is used in the singular it does not presuppose that there is only one leader in a church, indeed rather the reverse. Nor does it imply the male gender: I have not used inclusive language consistently because it can become wearisome, but there is certainly no implication that leaders can only be men.

Management studies

The idea of management as a subject to be analysed goes back to the turn of the nineteenth century. Alexander Hamilton (1757–1804) and the French economist J. B. Say (1767–1832) laid some of the foundations; but a century ago it began to burgeon with the growth of the large corporation in North America and Europe.[16] In its early days great hopes were held out for 'scientific management'. F. W. Taylor in 1911 went so far as to claim, 'it will mean, for the employers and the workmen who adopt it, the elimination of almost all causes for dispute and disagreement between them'.

Since then it has moderated its claims, and become a necessary tool of modern industry. Like any area of study it has its fads and fancies. 'Ideas can be compared to radioactive substances: they decay in potency and lose their lives over a period of time . . . therefore new ideas are essential to prevent ossification and sterility.'[17] A generation ago Management by Objectives swept the board and all were being urged to set quantifiable goals. Nowadays MBO is *passé*, and more subtle techniques are suggested. For this reason alone the church would be as foolish to follow only one theory in management studies as one school in philosophy. It would be equally imprudent to ignore the work which has been done, for the local church is a gathering of individuals and responds in much the same way as any other human group.

It is sometimes said that the church is a voluntary organisation and does not operate in the same way as a company with paid employees. While it is true that there are differences, much the same principles apply. For example, it is much more difficult to get rid of obsolete structures and people in a voluntary organisation: as Peter Drucker says, 'Most innovations in public-service institutions are imposed upon them by outsiders or by catastrophe.'[18] However, the principles whereby you may discover obsolesence are the same in both. It has also to be remembered that the church is only partly a voluntary organisation – it is a mixture of those who are paid and those who are voluntary, and this sets up its own tensions.

Moreover management theory is not an exact science. Like other human studies it has therefore tended to discover what seems to work in practice and then unearth the reasons why. This has its dangers. A doctor may be happy to give a pill which produces short-term benefits, but if the way it works is unknown it may lead to long-term disaster. Peter Drucker, an Austrian now living in the USA, has written voluminously on business studies for many decades, but has to say about his chosen subject, 'the emphasis is on techniques rather than principles, on mechanics rather than on decisions, on tools rather than on results, and, above all, on the efficiency of the part rather than the performance of the whole'.[19] The church must beware of pragmatism. To adopt something 'because it seems to work' can be as dangerous as prescribing thalidomide.[20]

But it is impossible to evade theory. Every decision we take, every approach we make to a problem, rests on assumptions, hypotheses and expectations, i.e. on theory. Often these fundamental beliefs are quite unconscious but they determine how we tackle a situation and what we anticipate will happen because of our action. Practice and theory are inextricable. It is as important for a leader to examine the roots of his own method of working as it is essential for the pastor to discern the reasons behind his own emotions.

Many of these presuppositions are theological. As early as 1937 Van Vleck, in his study *Our Changing Churches: a study in leadership*, said, 'often a minister is so convinced of the divine nature of the pattern he employs that he does not realise it rests upon certain assumptions about human nature which may no longer be valid'. He went on to show that the 'priestly' approach depends upon certain views of the nature of God and the church, and the unimportance of this world. In 1968, in *Ministry and Management*, Peter Rudge developed this in great detail in relation to what he saw as the five possible kinds of church structure and the appropriate leadership pattern for each.[21] Our theology should undergird our leadership, though it has to be said that very frequently ministers with very different theological perceptions end up with churches structured and run in very much the same way. The House Churches and the Roman Catholic churches are not as far apart as they would expect to be, although they may have arrived at the same solution by different routes. This suggests that the constraints of our culture and the oddities of human nature are more compelling than we care to admit. This in turn suggests that we shall need to look carefully at these factors.

There are no prizes for sloppiness of thinking in the Kingdom of God and we should be prepared to consider carefully what management theory can teach us, without adopting all its thinking or practice. This book sees management as an art rather than an exact science. But art is not purely intuitive. It is based on experience, observation and thought. A painter has to study the rudiments of her craft, examine her past work critically, learn from what others have done, and ponder her subject. So should any Christian leader.

When Paul said to the church in Rome that those with the charism of leadership should exercise it *en spoude* he was using a word rich in meaning (Rom. 12:8). It has about it the sense of urgency: leadership is not a dilettante subject, it must be rooted in actuality. *En spoude* also emphasises the importance of careful thought and study: the subject deserves more than a casual glance. The fact that the word carries overtones of 'anxious concern' will come as no surprise to any Christian leader.

But there is always a danger that a book on leadership will concentrate on the leader and forget the *people* who are his or her responsibility. It is therefore with them that we must begin.

1

Look at the People

'Take authority for the work and ministry . . .' The sonorous words of the bishop roll round the cathedral, the climax of many years during which each candidate has gone through a tense selection procedure, and a long training. The relatives look on, some excited and thankful to God, others uncomprehending and apprehensive.

Nothing speaks more loudly of the chasm between clergy and laity than an ordination service. Afterwards the ordained are thought of as never quite the same again. They are a little separate, a little unusual. The whole service says 'here are people entering a special caste'. Hereafter they will even be called by a title, 'The Reverend', which sets them apart from the rest of humanity. No lay ministry has anything like the same rigour about it except those who are called to full-time service akin to ordination – the religious life, the missionary. Nor is this differentiation confined to churches which have an episcopal form of government, it is as common in the non-episcopal churches. Even in the house churches leaders are regarded as somewhat different and more important than the rest. Whatever the Bible says about equal status before Christ, the practice says something wholly different.[1]

It is not therefore surprising that nearly all that is written about leadership in the church speaks primarily about the leaders rather than the led. This is by no means confined to the church. Very little work has been done recently on the place of the worker in the business organisation. Books pour off the presses on the role and work of the manager, but most of the work on industrial physiology was done in the 1900s,

11

industrial psychology was worked at in the 1910s, and there have been few studies on relationships on the factory floor during the last 30 years. Matters have been considered from the viewpoint of the executive in his office, and this has led to dangerous generalisations about the nature of organisations and how they work.

No Christian with a clear view of the argument of 1 Corinthians 12:12–26 with its concern for the interrelation and equal importance of each part of the Body of Christ can be happy with this situation. The Church of England Report, *A Strategy for the Church's Ministry,*[2] is right when it says: 'The status of any Christian is not in bearing the office of a priest, or a churchwarden, or an organist, but being by God's gift a baptised member of the laity.' Paul goes out of his way to stress, not that there is a mathematical parity of status (for he does not think in those terms), but that each ministry is 'indispensable' to every other ministry. This is not a call for democracy within the church where each person's voice has equal weight – I suspect such a suggestion would have horrified Paul – but that each ministry must be equally respected and used.

The church is not only theologically inept when its practices proclaim the depth of the clergy–lay divide, it is also foolish. The church is, in organisational terms, a voluntary association. Its members can join or leave at will, and although it may speak of the permanence of Christian discipleship, the reality in terms of membership of a local church is often very different. Since all in a church are volunteers, leadership is 'with the consent of the governed. The leadership works for the people and not vice versa'.[3] If people feel that their own contribution is neglected and played down then they will drift away and cease to play an active part. Common sense tells us that everyone should be honoured and valued both for themselves and for the future of the local organisation.

However, there is more to leadership than merely keeping people content and fulfilled. It is also particularly important to

keep the congregation at the forefront of the leader's thinking
in two other areas: teaching and mission.

Because of the skew by which leaders tend to see things
through their own eyes, the pulpit is seen as more important
than the pew. I am eternally grateful for someone who said to
me when I was talking about the teaching ministry of the
church, 'Are you sure you mean teaching – don't you mean
learning?' He was quite right. 'Unless there is someone who
hears, there is no communication. There is only noise.'[4] It is
always instructive to ask people what they can remember about
a sermon. Very seldom can they recall the three carefully
crafted points of the preacher; at worst all that can be recalled
is an anecdote or even some mannerism of the speaker. At
best they have remembered a point which has set their own
thinking in motion and which they have mulled over: it is
almost as though the Holy Spirit said, 'This is the Word of God
for you today.' That is why what the hearers often remember
is not even in the sermon for it is the result of their own
thoughts. Therefore if a teacher forgets to listen to his audience
he has forgotten his primary purpose of communication. The
question has to be constantly asked: 'Is what I am saying within
my hearer's range of perception?'

Mission is primarily the action of God in the congregation
not the leader. Facts bear this out. When people are asked,
'What is the main factor under God which led to you becoming
a Christian?' up to 80% will say, 'Through a one to one
encounter with a Christian.' Studies have shown that only 13%
will say that it was through an evangelistic event, and even
fewer through listening to a minister's sermon.[5] Therefore if
we concentrate on the leader and see him or her as the prime
agency for mission we shall fail to recognise God's main
method: his people. Furthermore we shall have church-centred
evangelism rather than a world-centred mission. Evangelism
then becomes a series of commando raids into enemy territory
to capture a few prisoners, rather than the extension of the
Kingdom in the life of individuals and the community.

Yet there is more. The Bible speaks throughout of the

majesty of the individual 'in Christ'. Ephesians sees this in cosmic terms: God 'chose us in Christ before the creation of the world', and 'raised us up with Christ and seated us with him in the heavenly realms' (Eph. 1:4; 2:6). Christ speaks with tender and yet fierce love of his 'little ones', to harm whom brings retribution beyond imagining (Mark 9:42). If those in leadership in the Church fail to recognise the precious treasure in their care they will indeed be the false shepherds of Ezekiel 34 who 'cared for themselves rather than for my flock'. It is not easy for the church leader looking on a Sunday morning at what an Anglican bishop recently called the 'collection of saints and fatheads' who make up an average congregation, to see beneath the surface to the beauty of what Christ has done through the cross as renewed lives are made whole in him. Paul could do it: when he wrote to the disturbed and disturbing church at Corinth he looked beneath the apparent chaos to the reality of the faith of its members, 'in him you have been enriched in every way' (1 Cor. 1:4–9).

Paul Minear lists no fewer than 96 different images for the Church which occur in the New Testament. He groups them under four heads, each a reminder of the greatness of the inheritance of the Christian:

(1) 'the people of God' stresses the way in which God has worked with a people throughout the history of faith, and that today's Christians are heirs of this great procession;
(2) 'the new creation' sees the Christian as someone who is bursting through into a new world, freed from the shackles of sin and self and able to dream new dreams and see wider horizons;
(3) 'the fellowship of faith' gives to the Christian forgiveness and joy through the cross and the life of Christ;
(4) 'the Body of Christ' is the corporate side of being 'in Christ', belonging to the Church of the living God, with all that means of love and of the breaking down of barriers.[6]

If leaders fail to see the members of their congregations with these biblical eyes they will inevitably be frustrated and confused. Christ looked at the crowd and, feeling a deep compassion (*splanchnizo*)[7] for them, saw an opportunity for his Father's grace to be seen in action. His disciples looked at the same people at the same time and only saw a problem (Mark 8:1–4). In practical terms this often means the 'difficult' person is seen as a problem rather than an opportunity. Admiral Hyman Rickover even saw the incorporation of such people as a test of the validity of an organisation, for it 'must somehow make room for inner-directed, obstreperous, creative people, sworn enemies of routine and the status quo, always ready to upset the apple cart by thinking up new and better ways of doing things.'[8] There were some among the apostles, for Christ saw their inner value rather than their apparent awkwardness.

The sin of reification

It is often said that one of the faults of our age is to see people as conglomerations rather than individuals. This is particularly true of those we dislike, whether it be 'the proletariat' or 'Wall Street', 'commies' or 'Thatcherites'. The danger is that we can shuffle off responsibility more easily; the Third World is a less beckoning symbol than a starving child. This is the process of 'reification', ascribing to a social group thoughts and actions which only an individual can have.[9] The church is not immune. To say of a certain church, 'it is traditional', does no more than say that certain individuals within the church hold certain conservative views. Within that church there will be many different opinions in the traditional–radical spectrum: there may be more at one end of the scale than the other but it is far from monochrome. When visiting a church I have often made the mistake of categorising it in my mind and being surprised when individuals have not conformed to my stereotype. This has to be borne in mind when we come to discuss different church structures, for it is too easy to judge a church as a single construct rather than an amalgam of different individuals.

Management studies also tend to reify. David Silverman points out the distinction that is often made between the 'transcendental', where an organisation is studied without reference to the people who are in it, and the 'immanent', where the individual is taken into consideration.[10] This use of theological words such as 'transcendental' and 'immanent' is startling but not inappropriate. The immanence of God, seen supremely in the Incarnation, is to do not only with the world but also with each person. It proclaims that the God of the galaxies is also God of the atom, that he cares for each, and each has its own place in his will.

For the Christian leader there is spiritual danger in reification. It is easier, because further from reality, to think in terms of the 'congregation' or the 'community' rather than Mrs Jones or Mr Smith. The pastoral ministry to individuals has always been a good corrective to this way of thinking, and it must be high on the list of priorities for the leader. It has its own particular dangers if it is seen as the whole of ministry, but it is neglected at the leader's peril. Airy generalisations about the congregation can feed a sense of self-importance. There is a balance between looking after the flock and tending each sheep.

People-orientated or task-orientated?

But a church is not just a mechanism for looking after its congregation. It has a task: in its widest terms this is the living and sharing of the Gospel. But this overall task breaks down into many particular items, which may range from building a church extension to establishing a youth club.

In the early 1960s the Tavistock Institute differentiated between the 'technical' and 'social' aspects of an organisation. The technical side produces goods, services, research, etc. But there is more to a widget factory than producing widgets. There is a complex social structure. This in its turn is both 'formal' and 'informal'. The formal is the part found on management charts: the subordinate–superior relationship, the peer level, and so on. However in many ways the morale and productivity of a business is set at least as much by the informal structure: the friendship groups, the discussions in the canteen, the casual chat in the car park.[11]

A church is the same. It too has a technical part, a task to be performed: services to be taken, people to be cared for, mission to be attempted. It also has a social structure, both formal and informal. Leaders tend to be concerned with the formal: the organisations and groups which exist within the church and which are set out on the notice-board. They may well see the smooth running of these as one of their primary jobs, but like businessmen they tend to forget the influence which is wielded by friends getting together over coffee or chatting after a meeting. The morale and enthusiasm of a church are determined largely by these informal interactions.

There has been much work done on the relative importance of the technical and social aspects of an organisation, for no successful modern management would forget the social aspect. But the relationship between the two is complex.

In 1962 Robert Blake and Jane Mouton produced a 'managerial grid' which has been widely adapted, and used in many different fields.[12] One manager may show a high degree of concern for people but pay little heed to producing anything. Another may be concerned only with 'the bottom line' and be cavalier in dealing with individuals in his way. By custom the graph has been drawn with axes of nine points. Hence the first manager would be in the 1,9 area, while the task-orientated slave-driver would be 9,1. The best manager would show a high concern both for people and for the task and score 9,9.

Churches, like any other social organisation, operate by the same rules and have the same pressures on the leadership. The 'good fellowship' or 'hospital' pattern of 1,9 represents a church where the leadership spends much time in keeping people happy. It has been described as an 'oilcan ministry'. If there is

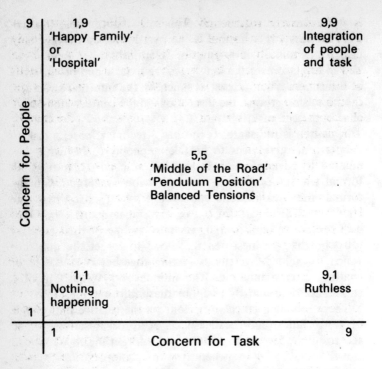

Fig. 1

the slightest squeak in the church the leader is expected to pour oil immediately on the situation. The fellowship attracts those who are all too conscious of their own needs, and want a group which will feed their hypochondria. For this reason it often has the atmosphere of a hospital ward. It is, however, highly dangerous, for such a warm inward-looking friendliness is bought at a price. Such a church welcomes everyone – provided they do nothing to upset the spurious warmth. Its evangelism welcomes only the like-minded. A leader who does what people want is canonised, while one who seeks to give vision and direction is accused of 'causing division' and vilified.

The ruthless 9,1 pattern, which has little regard for people, is unfortunately surprisingly common among churches. A leader who wants to impose his will – to make his church 'truly Catholic', 'soundly evangelical', 'fully charismatic' or even 'safely Anglican' – can ride roughshod over the spiritual needs of the congregation. Even worse is the minister who sees the church as a stage upon which he may strut. I heard one member of a congregation say scathingly of her minister and the church, 'It's his ego-show.'

It is not only self-seeking goals which can lead to a 9,1 inhumanity. There are right tasks as well as wrong, and the way in which a leader determines those which are right and carries them out is one of the most important areas of work. However all leaders must remember that they can forget and hurt people by an exclusive concentration on the task, even if it is the right one.

Nor does it only apply to the leader. A church which is more concerned about maintaining its own organisation or even survival is not caring for people. A congregation which refuses to think about mission is showing exactly the same hard-heartedness by disregarding the people in the community around the church. The adoption of such a standpoint usually leads, both in a business and in a church, to short-term gains and long-term losses. People are prepared to follow for a while but eventually rebel against being exploited and sabotage the task.

Of particular interest in Figure 1 is the diagonal from 0,0 to 9,9. Obviously 0,0 represents a church which has fallen asleep; it neither cares for people nor for achieving anything. 5,5 is often seen. It is sometimes described as the 'dampened pendulum' position, where there are shifts around a particular position. The church seeks to move in a certain direction and complete the tasks which God has set before it, but the expressions of pain from people in the congregation and the demands they make ensure that nothing is carried through. Some churches show the same characteristic symptoms of being in a 5,5 position as businesses. First, they seek to cater for everyone, not out of pastoral concern, but to keep people reasonably satisfied. There is, therefore, a multiplicity of organisations and services to cater for the needs of all. Secondly they tend to live by 'drives' on certain issues: it may be increased evangelism one month, followed by financial economies the next, and all run alongside a course on personal counselling. These special efforts tend to come, not from a true assessment of the situation, but because a crisis has surfaced, or a new idea has come from the latest book the minister has read or conference he has attended. The 'push' achieves little. The unresolved tensions in the church soon pull the pendulum back to its usual position. This classic 'middle-of-the-road' attitude seeks to get something done yet keep people moderately happy at the same time. It has to be recognised that this 'balanced' position, where the conflicting forces in a church are held in a position of tension, is comfortable in theory but in practice difficult and exhausting, and achieves little. In a tug-of-war sixteen brawny men try to pull a handkerchief a few feet. There are many churches like this.

This 5,5 position is particularly difficult for the leader, who is the recipient of much hostility. There tends to be much grumbling and it is directed at the leader. There are some who are saying 'more ought to happen' in the church, while others are crying out for personal ministry. It is for this reason that short-term drives are as much as he can manage. After they have run their course a period of 'consolidation' is needed to satisfy the clamant personal needs of individuals. In the 5,5 position the minister feels like the rope in the tug-of-war. The tensions in the church go through his heart.

The 9,9 position seeks to maximise both achievement and care for people. This position does not differentiate too minutely between the two, since if the church is under the control of God it will both achieve its appointed task and care for people. Fulfilment of the task will in itself care for the needs of many. Their morale is built up as they are helped by the church in their basic task of mission. The minor bruises of personal relationships are met with a laugh rather than a frown, and personal problems become less insistent. The mutual encouragement, the fellowship and the level of spiritual life increase when something is accomplished together. I have often noticed that even a successful fund-raising campaign will have this effect, let alone a successful mission or other real impact on the community. Christ's ministry to his disciples did not allow a mere balancing of tensions. He looked for far more than they thought they were capable of and set goals before them which made their eyes shine with the glory of it all. The 9,9 style sets tasks in which people can find a sense of personal worth and fulfilment, and challenges them to go further than they have ever been before. Much is expected and therefore much support needs to be given. Failure is not regarded as disgraceful but as inevitable from time to time if a person is moving into unknown territory. A mistake is used as a stepping stone to something higher.[13] The church becomes a body of people moving together on a common task, and fellowship and pastoral care are a very real but incidental bonus.

Long ago I ran many a youth group. For some reason I thought young people enjoyed long walks, and I would march them up a local mountain. I noted that at the bottom of the climb all were divided: some wanted to sit down, others scampered ahead, while others complained bitterly about their blisters and their companions. However, when the summit was in sight the mood changed. They wanted to get to it. Their pace quickened, they stopped grumbling, they helped each other. They had moved from 5,5 to 9,9. As leader I passed from being highly unpopular to being at least tolerated for my eccentricities, and youth leadership which had seemed to be total disaster became a wonderful opportunity for Christian witness.

X or Y or ?

In 1960 Douglas McGregor suggested that there were two ways in which a manager can view a worker. Either he adopted theory X and assumed that people dislike work, need to be driven to achieve anything, and are basically lazy. They respond to a carrot and stick approach. Or he could espouse theory Y which assumes that people want to achieve, and are capable of acting in an adult way and taking responsibility.[14] It seems at first glance that theory Y must be preferable in any humane organisation. But there are many caveats against adopting too readily a theory Y method of working.

First, and most obvious, people do not work in the same way all the time. They may be lazy when engaged on one job, enthusiastic on another. They may even be lazy one day and motivated the next while doing the same job. Every Christian leader has known moments of bewilderment when some trusted member of the congregation has 'let me down'.

Secondly and less obviously, theory Y is bad news for the vulnerable. Abraham Maslow even criticised it for its 'inhumanity' to those who cannot achieve the self-discipline, and ability to take the responsibility for their own self-command, which is required by theory Y.[15] Someone with little self-confidence may be unable to cope with an open agenda and with work which must be self-motivated. They may well find that it leads to failure and even lower self-esteem.

Thirdly, whiile theory X is at least open in its control of people, theory Y can be just as manipulative but in a more subtle way. While managers who use theory Y language talk in terms of 'self-fulfilment' and 'personal creativity' they tend to use psychological methods of manipulation which can be at least as directive as the orders barked out by the theory X manager.

Is there no other way? Is the Christian leader restricted either to ordering people about or leaving them to make their own mistakes and thereby reinforcing the lack of self-worth of the weak? There has to be another way, which perhaps we should call theory Z. The difficulty with both theory X and theory Y is that they look at the matter primarily from the point of view of the manager. If we are seeking to put the people first, then their needs and well-being must be our primary concern.

A 'theory Z' leader will realise that people need different

encouragements at different times for them to grow in Christ and achieve much for the Kingdom. There are times when a theory X approach is necessary for certain people. I can well remember when, at a time of personal crisis, an adviser gave me three straight instructions which he told me to follow. He was right: I needed that clarity from a trusted Christian leader. At other times we need to encourage people's *enkrateia*, which can be translated 'self-control' or 'sense of responsibility'.[16] Part of the task of the Christian leader is to help each one for whom he is responsible to develop their potential in Christ. This often means pushing them a little further than they have previously been, into those 'faith-stretching situations' where they will learn to rely upon the Lord working through them.

A leader should not see people as either lazy or self-motivated, but as infinitely variable and worthwhile. The leader will be fundamentally optimistic about human nature redeemed by Christ, while being well aware of the depths of sin and the possibility of falling. Above all the leader will not manipulate for his or her own ends – to use people in this way does not become one who is called to be 'the servant of the servants of God'.

Why do people come to church?

We need undertake no more than a most cursory self-examination to realise that not everyone goes to church purely to worship God, to hear his Word, and receive his Sacrament. The wonder is that God takes our mixed motivations and uses them in his Kingdom. People came to Christ for many different reasons – curiosity, superstition, greed – and he accepted them as they were. We shall have a clearer view of the members of the congregation if we look at the possible reasons for people being in the pews. Leaders are often puzzled why some members of the congregation are deeply committed to God and to the local church while others are perfunctory or variable.

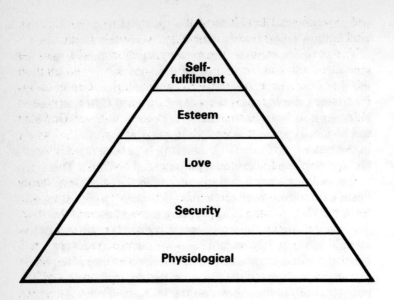

Fig. 2

If we examine their possible motivations we may see more clearly why this is so.

Abraham Maslow constructed a triangle to illustrate the different needs of a human being. He called it the 'hierarchy of needs'. It has been much criticised[17] and Maslow himself warned us not to take it too seriously but it makes a useful starting point.

Physiological needs are those of basic survival – food and air and water. It is unlikely that many people in the western world go to church for these reasons today, but they certainly did in the not too distant past when it was the welfare agency for the poor and sick. Until quite recently in Britain a man's job might depend on his being in church on Sunday. However in the last couple of decades there has been a significant development. The growing emphasis upon the healing ministry has meant that the church is seen as seeking to meet the need for physical and psychological health as well as pastoral care. Once again God is seen as interested in meeting these basic needs.

The need for *security* brings many to church. The world is seen as hostile and the church as a haven. Some who think in this way wish to see no change in the existing pattern of things for to them the church spells safety and warmth and a place to hide. As a lady in Newcastle said to me, 'Without God and this church, I would fall apart.' Those who wish to find safety in the church will often be enthusiastic about small groups, social events, and a 1,9 'happy fellowship' pattern.

We all have a need for *love* and acceptance. In the church this is expressed through fellowship and personal ministry, and we hope that through this people will come to see that they are accepted in the Beloved, though we are conscious that it is often difficult to wean people away from dependency on a person to a reliance upon God: if this transference is not made then any breaking or cooling of the human relationship will be likely to result in only spasmodic attendance. This is often seen after a minister leaves a church: those he particularly nurtured no longer feel as close to the centre of things and drift. The friendship a church can provide means that there is a network of relationships, sexual and otherwise, which can be valuable to all. In particular the lonely and the heavy-laden can find support and enrichment of their lives: it is for this reason that so many members of a congregation are of this kind.

'You shall love your neighbour *as yourself*.' The need for *esteem* is important. Many find their status within the life of the church; holding an official position is a great part of their feeling of self-worth. Where they see this as something given by God and for which they are answerable to him, all is healthy. But it is easily distorted into a self-regard based upon the holding of a position in the church.[18] That is why it is all too often true that after people relinquish office they drift away from the fellowship because their reason for belonging has disappeared.

It is said that most users of computers use only 5% of the power of which their machines are capable. In the same way we use only a small proportion of what God has given us. We all need to move into wider pastures where we can find a degree of *self-fulfilment*. Faith pushes us into areas which we would not normally dare to enter, and there is great joy for a leader in hearing someone say, 'If you had told me a year ago that I would do that, I'd have laughed in your face'. The church can release hidden creativity, from the flower arranger and the banner maker to the dramatist and the musician. But it is not only in the more obviously artistic areas that new possibilities occur. People discover gifts, sometimes latent all their lives, sometimes newly God-given. They may find a capacity for helping people, for organising events, for speaking, for 'flowing with the Spirit'.

These five motivations are earthbound. Above and beyond them is the human *desire for God*. The restlessness of the heart for its Maker has to be met. A church which only fulfils human needs cannot wholly satisfy. It must communicate the being of God in a way which is both real and accessible.

We are more 'rice Christians' than we care to admit – members of our local church for what we can get out of it. Few these days may attend for material gain, but other needs may well be met through such an organisation. The danger is that once the needs which brought us have been satisfied, or are met in some other way, then our membership will decline and we will become at best an occasional member. If someone's need for love and fellowship is met through some new experience, such as joining a Rotary or Working Men's club, then the church has served its purpose and is no longer needed. This fact makes even more important the need to preach the Gospel to those who are within the church as well as those who are outside, for there are 'many passengers who should be pilgrims', as Archbishop Runcie has said.[19] There can be no long-term loyalty and commitment to a church unless people are able to see it as leading them to the Throne and doing more than fulfilling their needs as human beings.

As Christian leaders we should be both aware of the motivations of the people before us and able to lead them further.

If we merely meet those needs we shall be well liked but pastorally incompetent. Sometimes the needs have to be challenged; e.g. we should question anyone whose faith is totally bound up in the church office he holds. Sometimes we should gently suggest new prospects for the shy and new possibilities for the apparently stolid.

But if the leader thinks that on Sunday morning the people in front of him are there only because they have come to worship God and hear his Word he dwells in fantasy land.

The shape of the church

Leaders who are geared to think primarily of the congregation will have a different attitude from those who concentrate on their own leadership and the running of the church organisation.

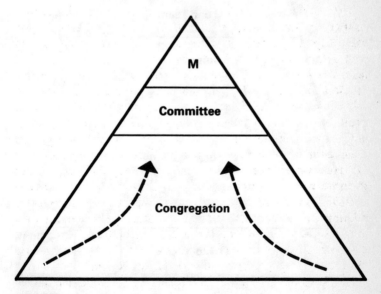

Fig. 3a

The traditional pattern (Fig. 3a) can be thought of as a triangle. The minister is seen as being at the apex, with all the lines of authority and importance flowing in his or her direction. Clearly the leader cannot do all the work so others are called in to help with the task. Hence the formation of church councils and committees. As John Betjeman said:[20]

> For P.C.C.s were really made
> To give your local Vicar aid.

Such a pattern of thinking is inevitably going to result in a church which is self-contained, for all the lines of force within it are internal. On occasion it can reach out in some form of mission, but it is not a natural activity for such an organisational structure, therefore mission seems rather forced and strange, and tends to be sporadic and the work of a few 'enthusiasts'.

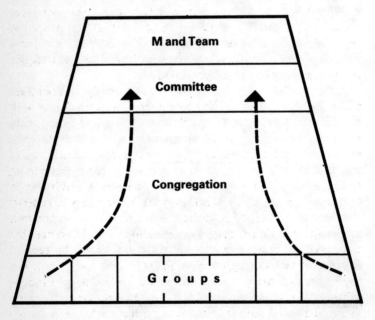

Fig. 3b

The congregation in this model is almost encouraged to be passive and to 'pay up and shut up'.

A second pattern (Fig. 3b) occurs when a church becomes more aware of the gifts of the congregation and wishes to make use of them. But these gifts are thought of as being used almost exclusively within the framework of the church. Those with gifts of leadership are especially prized and are called upon to share in the task of leading the church. In this pattern leadership is even more important than in the previous model. The leader has to be not only the focus of the congregation but also the chairman of a team, with all the tensions which that brings. Although there may be a great deal of activity with a multitude of house groups and other sub-organisations, the main thrust of the church is still internal. Once again the congregation is seen as basically there to support the leadership, and although there may be a greater willingness to think in terms of mission it still tends to be foreign to a structure with stress upon the 'event' rather than on the everyday mission of the people of God. This second model is healthier than the first, but it can be enormously activist and demanding of the time and energies of the members of the congregation.

A third pattern (Fig. 3c) is possible. It is simply to take either model and turn it upside down. This is more easily done with the second model because people in such a church are already more conscious of the need to think ahead, than with the first model where the rather passive congregation has not taken responsibility for the life of their church and leaves everything to the leader. This simple operation denotes a revolution in thinking for many leaders. It means that their role is to support and enable the ministries of the congregation both within and, especially, outside the church organisation. The difference that this makes to leadership styles is profound, as will be seen in later chapters. Although at first glance it looks as though this model imposes more burden on the leaders, in fact the load is lightened because the whole responsibility no longer rests on them, and the church is less dependent. It enables the church council to see their function as more than keeping the organis-

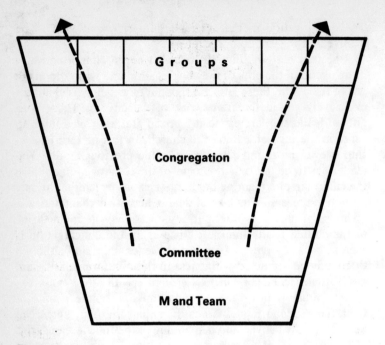

Fig. 3c

ation going and the minister in check, and widens their vision to see how they can help the members of the congregation to come into their own. Further, the congregation see themselves as important in the life of the church and their ministries are valued and encouraged. Groups and organisations look outwards rather than inwards, with a lessening of an excessively intense cell-centred life. Above all this model produces a people who push outwards in mission and upwards in worship. As one old Methodist miner said to me when he saw this diagram: 'Eh, lad, it's a flower pot' – and so it is.

The leaders provide the soil and nutriments which enable the plant to grow and flower outside the confines of the pot. The whole congregation looks outwards rather than inwards and the church is seen for what it is, a beautiful flowering tree

Fig. 3d

which blooms in the desert places (a picture which is often applied to the people of God):

> Israel will bud and blossom
> and fill all the world with fruit.

> (Is. 27:6)

It should be emphasised that these models, like all such, should be treated with caution. They do not represent different structures or methods of church government. Rather they illustrate different ways of perceiving a church. There will not be only one, uniform model in the minds of people who belong to a particular church. Even when the leadership of a church is striving to operate under the third model, there will be plenty of people in the congregation who are still thinking in terms of the second or even the first model. In particular the great majority of people outside the church will still come to the minister for everything because they automatically think in terms of the first model.

Of particular difficulty is the way in which churches are seen by other structures, including ecclesiastical ones. The first model is neat and easily grasped, and conforms most closely to what is imagined to be the normal structure of a hierarchical organisation. When this is written down in legislation, whether in statute or canon law, change can be difficult to effect. The Church of England is especially hamstrung by this, for all such matters as the freehold, and the legal concept of the corporation sole, are essentially of this model.

Nevertheless there is a rightness about the 'flower-pot church' which makes it an ideal towards which to work. It is the only model which sees the church as a means and not as an end, for when the church is seen as an objective in itself it has become an idol. If the church's main aim and priority is its own life, it has ceased to be a 'tool in the hand of the living God' and has become just another organisation.

The flower-pot church is essentially reaching *upwards* and *outwards*. Upwards it is reaching towards the being of God. As Niebuhr said, 'Nothing less than God – albeit God in the mystery of his being as Father, Son and Holy Spirit – is the object towards which Scriptures, Church and Jesus Christ himself direct those who begin by loving him.'[21] A church which is seeking this sort of worship will be encouraging its members to approach God in various ways – the many, wonderful paths by which we may come into the holy of holies. It will not try to force people to follow only one or two ways, for it will be thinking about its members and how they may appreciate and love God most appropriately for themselves.[22] In such a church there will be no 'party line' which means that those who follow a certain path (Evangelical, Tractarian or whatever) are 'in' and those who follow another are 'out'. Josephine Bax was asked to travel widely in England and find out what the overall position of renewal was in the Church of England. One of the main features of her book *The Good Wine* (1986) was the multiplicity of different ways in which she found God is working. There seems to be only one factor which is common to all: the preparedness to take the risks of faith and step into areas previously unknown.

A model three church will also look outwards. Inevitably if we follow one who came 'to save the world' we should look outwards at the world in its need of salvation. Each member of the congregation is in the world and it is in support of their mission that much of the church's ministry must be given. Where evangelism and social action are concerned, as was said long ago, 'we have got to mean business, but let us not get too grim about it'. That last phrase is important. Too much mission has a flavour of earnest endeavour or guilt-ridden effort: we are asking people to join in the dance of life more abundant.

This chapter is a marker. Although we shall be thinking much about the role of the leader we shall try to remember that he only operates within a context – and that frame of reference is the congregation. Without them he is a general without an army or a social worker without clients. We shall also be looking at ways in which the leader can enable a church to become a 'flower pot' which seeks to fulfil the ministries of the members of the congregation. To begin with, we need to see them – and ourselves – as we are, as the Holy Spirit leads us into truth.

Conclusion

Certain questions come out of this chapter which may be useful for leaders to focus on as they look at the church to which they belong, and for which they are in some measure responsible:

(1) Where on the Blake and Mouton managerial grid is the prevailing cluster of opinion in your church?

(2) As a leader do you tend to theory X or theory Y in your handling of people? How can you move towards theory Z?

(3) Why do people come to your church? Examine the motivations of certain people in the congregation.

(4) Does your church need any change of attitude to turn it into a 'flower pot'?

(a) What is the prevailing 'model' in the minds of your congregation?

(b) How can model three be communicated to others, both individuals and groups?

(c) Which organisations and activities primarily serve the congregation and which support the church as an organisation?

(d) Can evangelism and social action be more closely related to the life experience of the members of the congregation? How can they be helped in this?

2

The Nature of Christian Leadership

What is leadership?

In my younger days I sat at the feet of a great preacher. I envied much his fluency, his spellbinding qualities, and his spiritual maturity. I copied the pattern of his sermons, his gestures, even his voice inflexion. It was some time before I emerged from his influence and developed my own ministry. Every great Christian leader trails behind him or her a cavalcade of copy-cats. These imitate the methods but cannot copy the thought, prayer and personality which brought the methods to birth. Similarly every famous church finds imitations springing up, copying the programmes which it has initiated, and failing to seek the Holy Spirit's guidance for their own churches. Great leaders and 'successful' churches can tempt others into an attempt to find 'the magic bullet', that programme or change of leadership style which will attain the same blessing from God. It is yet another example of 'cheap grace', a means by which we can grow without pain and without directly dealing with the living God.

What is a definition of 'leadership'? Those bold enough to attempt this tend to concentrate on the effectiveness with which the leader can manipulate others. Hence there are such definitions as: 'the capacity to harness human and other resources to achieve results' (Woodcock and Francis);[1] 'getting others to follow', 'deciding what ought to be done, and then getting other people to do it' (Stewart).[2]

Such definitions tend to emphasise the element of 'control', whereby one person influences the actions of another in a desired direction. But Christian leadership (and good business practice) is at least as much about enabling the ministries of other people to blossom as it is about getting them to do what we want.

Others define leadership in almost mystical terms – 'You know a leader when you meet one', 'You either have it or you haven't'. They believe that leaders are born with a silver spoon in their mouths which no one can take from them. Those taking this viewpoint are dismissive of those who they feel have not 'got it'. They reject the idea that leaders need to be trained: those who are imbued with 'leadership qualities' need no training, and those who do not have them cannot benefit from it.

It is important to tease out this question, for from the answer comes our understanding of leadership and the part it plays in the Christian church. It seems that in fact leadership is made up of several variables:[3]

(1) *The attitudes and needs of the people who are being led*. One Christian leader may be very much at home among people open to change in the heart of an industrial city and yet be unable to cope with a traditionally-minded church made up of doctors and lawyers. One leader I know has a magnificent ministry among the mentally handicapped which I and many others could not even begin to emulate. We cannot ignore the people we are set among. But it is not merely a matter of social context: it applies to the individual. One person may need one style of leadership and another person a different approach. Even more complicated is the fact that the same individual will need different leadership styles at different times. For example, young Christians often need a fairly directive style for a few months after they have come to faith, but to continue this style permanently will keep them as 'perpetual infants', where they never grow out of dependency – which is good neither for them nor the leader. This continuous change of leadership style is less complicated than it sounds. We are used to changing our social behaviour to suit the environment: we may speak in a

single hour to a baby, a bank manager and a bus driver, and use very different verbal and body language with each. A good leader does not need to be asking all the time 'What style of leadership does this person need from me?' but will move effortlessly and without much thought from one setting to another, bringing the appropriate style to each. A stereotyped approach to every person tends to indicate a leader who is unable to let his or her real self be seen, and so projects an artificial image.

(2) *The nature of the organisation.* A large urban church engaged in a major building project requires different leadership qualities to a poorly attended church set in the heart of the countryside. Communities have different goals and structures and a leader may be excited and effective in one and not in another. This is not just a matter of having appropriate skills for one environment and not for the other. We have a rapport with one situation which is lacking with another.

(3) *The prevailing culture.* Every age has its own political and social environment. It was said of one clergyman who clearly believed in benevolent autocracy, 'he should have been born in the nineteenth century'. We have to take into account the way in which people think and the motivations which drive them, and an understanding of these is one of the marks of a leader. But besides this overall culture there are many 'microclimates' such as a church, a miners' welfare club, a discussion group, or a school. Each has its own customs, preferences and social patterns, and the person who is a natural leader in one may be ineffective in another. I remember a most formidable hospital administrator, whose voice all obeyed, being unable to read the words set in front of her in a church service. Similarly I approach a church pulpit in a more comfortable frame of mind than when I am speaking to 600 comprehensive school pupils or a prison chapel full of inmates.

(4) *The personality of the leader.* There have been many attempts to discover the particular personality characteristics

which make for an effective leader. It would make the selection of candidates for leadership so much easier if we could make a shopping list of the attributes which we need to look for and then discard all who do not have them. Such lists have been drawn up by several researchers, but very few qualities are common to the various lists. This low correlation suggests that there is no single type of personality which can be designated 'leadership material'. There is some suggestion that intelligence, integrity, self-assurance and individuality are a help,[4] but even these are not essential. The fact remains that a person may be a leader in one situation and not in another.

Douglas McGregor concluded his examination of the nature of leadership: '[it] is not a property of the individual, but a complex relationship among these variables'. It is this that makes its study so rewarding, and enables a far greater number of people to take some leadership role than is often imagined.

For these reasons it is a gross oversimplification to say that a leader is 'born, not made'. A leader emerges from within a certain set of circumstances at a particular time. The context is all-important. A small group can often be instructive in providing a useful microcosm of a church or other larger assembly of people. So, within the ten people meeting as a house group, Mr Brown may lead the teaching, Mrs Pink may be looked to for spiritual awareness and Mr Gray will organise social events. Eddie Gibbs sums it up: 'Effective leadership depends on the right person being in the right place at the right time . . . it is both personal and contextual.'[5]

It follows that the selection and placing of the right person in the right place is an important part of the overall leadership of a church and much time and prayer should precede such a decision. Not the least difficulty is that the church is a voluntary association. This means it is much more difficult to get the wrong person out of a post than in a business concern where it is possible to move or even dismiss those who are inadequate. It is not surprising that Christ spent the night in prayer before choosing the twelve disciples.

But leadership is not only a matter of personality and context. First, Christian leadership is a charism of the Holy Spirit and we need to examine its nature. Secondly leadership needs to be trained.

Leadership as a charism from God

The word 'charism' is used with intent. The Greek word *charisma* is usually translated 'gift', but this suffers from a major defect which is particularly important when considering leadership. A gift, in ordinary speech, involves a transfer of ownership. If you receive a gift it is now yours, and the donor has no further rights over it: you may sell it or throw it away. But a spiritual 'charism' does not cease to be the possession of God. If it is to be wholesome it must be exercised under his constant guidance and in an overall atmosphere of love. If someone called and gifted by God as a leader fails to recognise this constant dependence upon the grace of God there is every danger that the 'gift' will be used for self-serving ends, and it is all too easy for leaders to feel that 'once I needed to depend upon God, but now I know how to do it'.[6] On the other hand, to use the straight transliteration *charisma* is no longer possible since it has become a jargon word signifying personal magnetism. The word 'charism', although not elegant, is exact and is used by many Roman Catholic writers (and the Second Vatican Council). A charism has been defined by Arnold Bittlinger as 'a gratuitous manifestation of the Holy Spirit working in and through, but going beyond, the believer's natural ability for the common good of the people of God'.[7]

A Christian leader does not just have to be the right person in the right place at the right time, he also has to be God-gifted. Indeed if a Christian leader has many natural abilities it is all too easy for him to follow his own way, use his personal gifts to be 'successful', and end by building a construction of 'wood, hay or straw' which will not survive into eternity.[8] Peter had to learn that his own enthusiasms were not the will of God, and many Christians down the ages have also found this a hard lesson. The trappings of 'successful' leadership – the respect of others, admiration, dependency – are a strong brew and not all have kept their heads. Christ's rebuke to the religious leaders of his day serve as a reminder that we should not do things 'for men to see', or love the 'place of honour' or to be 'greeted in the marketplace' (Matt. 23:1–12). Every natural talent and the whole of personality has to be offered to God and consecrated if it is to be useful in the Kingdom.

But is there a charism of leadership in the New Testament? It does not occur in so many words in the various lists of charisms to the church.[9] Yet it is clearly needed if the other charisms are to be coordinated and given direction. The only word which approximates to this function in the church is the word 'apostle'. This title stands at the head of the two lists of ministries set out most systematically in Ephesians and 1 Corinthians. The word is used to describe the Twelve, but also others: Paul especially, but such people as Barnabas, Andronicus and Junia as well. It has proved almost impossible for scholars to discover exactly what was meant by 'apostle' in New Testament times. Sometimes it appears to refer to leaders who had a missionary role as 'church-planters'. Once a church had been founded the apostle appeared to continue to exercise a particular authority over it; indeed the Pauline epistles themselves show one church-planter exerting that authority. On the other hand there are times when the word seems to mean little more than a delegate sent by one church to another, as in the case of Epaphroditus in Philippians 2:25. It seems likely that the word was used with a variety of meanings in different contexts. Further it is clear that nowhere is there any suggestion that the ministry of the apostle was intended only for the Christians of the first century.

But whatever the exact meaning of 'apostle' in New Testament times, there is a continuing need in every church for two kinds of authority. One is that exercised by some people in the *local* church to coordinate and encourage the gifts of others and to exercise discipline and oversight. The other is the *non-*

local authority which is needed because each local church is only a part of the whole catholic Body of Christ and that needs to be represented in its thinking. Both are matters of practical common sense, and both have emerged even in those denominations which have been fiercest in maintaining the rights of the local church. Virtually all newly founded churches have found that they have needed first a body of leaders, and later some reference point outside the local church. Whether or not these ministries derive from the concept of 'apostle' is debatable but the need for 'apostleship' in some form seems indisputable.[10]

That there is a charism of leadership is clear. It is easy to discuss the relationship of the leader to the rest of the congregation. It is less easy to realise that the all important relationship is that between the leader and his God. D. T. Niles described the leader as being caught up in a 'momentum apart from himself', and many leaders will identify the feeling of being out of control of their own ministry and being swept along in the purposes of God. The leader must share the heart and mind of God, identify with his will, and look at the world with his eyes. If we do not have this width of vision we shall become petty and parochial and pernickety. And this vision comes from God. Like the Old Testament priest the leader's role is to stand as a bridge between God and the people – praying for the people to God and explaining the ways of God to people.

The training of leaders

Whether leaders are born that way or emerge from a particular situation, their leadership potential can be increased. There are certain fields where training is particularly important:

(1) *Knowledge of self.* Leaders have to be aware of themselves as people and know what effect their actions have on others. Paul's injunction to 'think of yourself with sober judgement'[11]

is particularly important for those whose decisions affect many. Although they may have their limitations, personal questionnaires have their uses when done with the help of another person who knows us well.[12]

(2) *Expanding knowledge*. Leaders have to keep a flexibility of mind and approach to new problems. Mental arthritis does not have to be a sign of advancing years. Intellectual muscles need exercising. This may mean reading the latest books and theological periodicals, but in experience this area is one of great guilt for most ministers: they would like to read the scholarly volumes but find that their library is full of books with markers which never get beyond page 40. Reading may be important, but still more important is to think rigorously and theologically through the practical situations and problems which the everyday life of any church will present. The probing mind will always be seeking reasons for people's actions and better ways in which they can be helped. It will be seeking the will of God and following it, taking the vision and turning it into reality. One church did some research and found that two-thirds of the people in its house groups had left school as soon as was legally possible (at 13 for some of the older members). This made the leaders reflect on the sort of training material the groups were being asked to cope with and subsequently to alter the whole learning programme into something more appropriate.

There is a common feeling that this action-directed thinking is in some way inferior to academic learning, but it can be just as demanding and may be a good deal more use. The danger of unreflective leadership is that there is no careful deliberation about anything, and the church just responds unthinkingly to events as they occur. The result is a ministry which is purely reactive and never proactive, pushed and pulled by every pressure.

A leader needs wide experience and the ability to profit from it. It is sad when a leader retires from work after having spent a lifetime putting into operation only what he learnt in his first few years of ministry. We need a breadth of experience of different churches and denominations, and the widest legitimate knowledge of life. There is some evidence from industry that several moves in the early part of a person's career leads to a deeper treasure chest of experiences than if he or she has been confined to only one branch. Many firms deliberately move personnel for this among other reasons.

(3) *Knowledge of leadership skills*. A leader has to know about leadership. It may sound obvious, for after all, a doctor needs to know about medicine, and a lawyer about law. However there has been a great reluctance among those called to lead to learn the skills of their craft. This is as true in industry and the professions as in the life of the church, but much work has been done on management in recent years, and Christian leaders should not be too proud to learn from it. After all we use the knowledge of the psychologists in our counselling of people, and the designs of the architect in building a church extension.

The way in which such training can be acquired depends upon what needs to be learnt. Self-awareness can come about from days spent in prayer and discussion with a Christian friend or spiritual director. Leadership skills can be learnt from books and courses. Wider experience can come through a wisely used sabbatical, or a deliberate attempt to widen one's viewpoint. One church has taken this seriously and insists on the minister taking a whole Sunday off every two months in order to visit other churches and see how others worship: they say he comes back with freshness and new ideas, and they enjoy the visiting ministers or taking the services themselves.

What does a leader do?

Most books on management give lists of 'jobs for managers',[13] but it is at this point in particular that the scriptural base must be seen to be secure. What a manager does in a business is not necessarily what a Christian leader should be about. Christ

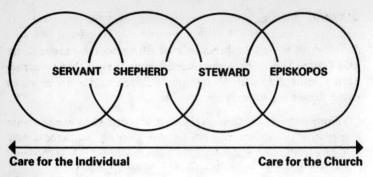

SERVANT SHEPHERD   STEWARD   EPISKOPOS

Care for the Individual   Care for the Church

Fig. 4

specifically warned about taking our leadership patterns from the outside world: 'Those who are regarded as rulers of the Gentiles lord it over them . . . not so with you.'[14]

The biblical pattern of leadership is complex but can be seen as being grouped around four words: Servant; Shepherd; Steward; *Episkopos*. Each word serves as a focus for a galaxy of other biblical ideas and titles, and they are not independent of each other. There is considerable overlap between them and it is impossible to fit each idea precisely into place. They can be seen as four interlocking circles. Each word lies on a continuum stretching from care for each person to concern for the corporate whole. As we shall see some of the hardest decisions in Christian leadership come from the tension between the various roles. For example a member of the congregation may be doing a job very badly. For the good of the whole Body of Christ it is best for that person to be removed from that work, but as minister you know that it will cause great pain. The *episkopos* says the member must go, while the servant/shepherd says that he or she must stay and the other members of the congregation learn a lesson in forbearance. Such decisions can tear the heart of any leader.

Servant

It is too easy for our biblical thinking to be overpowered by one very insistent image or epigrammatic saying. The towering verses in Mark 10:43–45 are part of the mental furniture of every Christian leader:

> Whoever wants to become great among you must be your servant [*diakonos*], and whoever wants to be first among you must be your slave [*doulos*]. For even the Son of Man did not come to be served but to serve, and to give his life as a ransom for many.

But while this is a great truth, it is important to recognise that there are more frequent references in the New Testament to the leader as a servant of *God* than there are to him or her as a servant of *people*. While a mere totting up of texts is not definitive it indicates that there is a balance which must be kept in mind. Otherwise the minister sees himself, and is seen by the congregation, as being at the beck and call of everyone's demands, and tries to fulfil the expectations of all. That way lies a subjugation of leadership to the democratic wishes of the people, or the tyranny of every manipulator in the congregation. Christ's primary task was to 'do his Father's work'; only secondarily was he a servant of the people.

There are a variety of 'servant' words, each of which shows us something of this role of the minister.

Doulos. Slave is the word from which we try to escape, for to be in bondage to another, to be under their control, is a fearful thing. Nor can we escape its meaning by saying that we are called to be the slave of God, and not of the congregation. The word used in Mark 10 is *doulos*. While it is true that if we see our ministry only in this way we shall lose our individuality and become the football of others, kicked from one end of the church to the other, it is nevertheless a truth which no leader of the people of God should evade.

The word 'slave' emphasises that the leader has to accept the negative forces of the congregation. He is the scapegoat on whom people heap their hostility and frustrations, and yet is supposed to lead them into freedom. If anything is perceived to be wrong the leader will receive the blame. And through it all the leader has to stand still and be beaten. If he or she cannot turn that maelstrom of negative emotion and thinking towards God then they will surely be submerged by it. This is particularly true of leaders who are highly affected by stress. They 'squander much of their energy being troubled about others' perceptions of them . . . those who manage stress well are not excessively disturbed if other people disapprove of them'.[15] This means that true *doulos* leaders have to have a right self-confidence, need to be aware of the reasons why hostility is coming their way, and above all, have a lively faith in the liberating power of the cross of Christ. Christ is our exemplar in this ministry. In 1 Peter 2:18–25 the writer starts with an exhortation to those who are slaves to bear with their lot, and ends with a general command to all Christians to copy the example of Christ, the innocent Suffering Servant, who 'entrusted [*paradidomi*, to hand over] himself to him who judges justly'. All leaders must learn that ability to 'hand over' – diverting the negative on to the Lord who bore all evil on the cross. If we take it as a personal attack, or allow it to sink into our soul, we shall either develop a protective shell which is cynical and bitter, or sink into a pit of self-pity which says 'nobody loves me, nobody understands me, nobody respects me'. We have also to remember that if we do not accept the negative then it will be directed elsewhere, probably towards our marriage partner, or another leader in the church.

The central fact of slavery is that a slave is not in control of himself. He can be set free or sold, flogged or cosseted at the whim of his master. But Paul gloried in the fact that this was not a forced servitude, but one willingly undertaken: 'Though I am free and belong to no man, I make myself a slave to everyone, to win as many as possible.' It is useful to remember that the word is used only twice in the sense of being a slave of *people* (in Mark 10 and 1 Cor. 9:19) and 18 times of being a slave of *God*. There will inevitably be times when the Christian leader is torn between obedience to God and the acceptance of the negative forces of other people. The former must take precedence for we are above all bearers of that title which Paul used so often, *Doulos Christou Iesou*.

Diakonos. This is an honourable title. It is enshrined in the three orders of ministry as the deacon, and is also common among non-episcopal denominations. It is one which accords well with the spirit of the mid-1980s – one who is the enabler, the resource person in the background, giving space in which other Christians can grow. If *doulos* primarily emphasises the relation of the servant to his master, *diakonos* emphasises the relation to his people: *doulos* is vertical, *diakonos* is horizontal.

In the later strands of the New Testament *diakonos* has already become an ecclesiastical title, and in 1 Timothy 3:8–13 there is a fairly detailed list of the requirements for those called to this office. Earlier the stress is on the *diakonos* as being the person who kept the wheels turning smoothly in the church. At times the *diakonos* is almost an administrator, while other passages suggest someone who is a sub-leader to whom others can turn with confidence. A leader working in this role will be within the church structure and will be referred to as a source of information and skills. If a church runs day to day with quiet efficiency it shows that the deacon role is being performed. If a church's morale is low because people have not received information, and the administration is poor, it indicates otherwise.

It has to be recognised that someone who is only fulfilling this role is not covering the whole span of leadership. A deacon-figure can run a comfortable, cosy, 1,9 church which is not speaking to the deepest needs of people, or providing any vision of the future. Leaders who are strong in this area tend to be good at administration and keeping people happy: they produce a lot of paper for internal information and are liked by their congregation. But by itself that is not enough. The vogue for the leader as being just an enabler of others is now passing, and the more robust areas of leadership are coming to the fore. But the unglamorous role of deacon is important and must not be neglected or the more vigorous leadership styles founder in a welter of poor communication and bewildered people.

Huperetes, therapon, leitourgos. The New Testament uses *doulos* 20 times in reference to Christian leaders and *diakonos* 23 times, and there are many references to their associated verbs. But there is also a clutch of words used much less frequently, each of which has its own flavour.

The *huperetes* was a rower on one of the lower banks of oars on a Greek ship. It was dirty, strenuous and dangerous work, and although the word had long been used more widely to describe any assistant worker, it still retained the idea of hard work. No Christian leader should be a slacker. *Huperetes* emphasises that leaders are *accountable* for their work – to God, to those in authority over them in the church, and to those whom they lead. The way in which accountability can be recognised is examined later in Chapter 5 but its importance is great.

There is only one use of the word *therapon* in the New Testament, and that describes Moses in Hebrews 3:5. The *therapon* was someone who assisted a doctor. We could probably translate it 'nurse' or 'orderly'. The work of the servant minister is to care for the hurts of people, to bind up the broken-hearted, and to arbitrate between those at variance. It was the work so often done by Christ in settling the divisions and quarrels among the disciples, and it is a ministry which we see Paul undertaking when he tried to bring Euodia and Syntyche together at Philippi and the various factions into harmony at Corinth.

The servant can too easily be overconcerned with the effect of his ministry on others and tend to become a cat's-paw of the needs of the congregation. The word *leitourgos* refers us back to God. It was used primarily of someone who served the state, what we would call a civil servant, but often in the New Testament it is used of a servant of God, particularly in the context of public worship. The English transliteration 'liturgy' reminds us of the 'sacrifice of praise' which is the Christian duty to God. The word is often used with sacrificial overtones, not least when Paul describes his own ministry in moving terms: 'I am being poured out like a drink-offering on the sacrifice and service coming from your faith.'[16]

In all discussions about the Christian leader as a servant the supreme example of the Servant has to be kept before our eyes, or we fail to see the importance of this role, or resent the placing of it on our shoulders. It is one which is often uncomfortable, not least to our pride and our ambition. It is one we prefer not to engage in. We need to consider Jesus who said, 'I am among you as one who serves'[17] – and bow in obedience.

Shepherd

The role of shepherd is the one in which most Christian leaders feel at home. They are trained to be pastors who care, guide and counsel. It is a role which does not have the uncomfortable feel of the servant or the potential for loneliness inherent in the idea of *episkope*. It is the traditional work of the Christian minister, and it is the one which is most expected by others. It has deep roots. Chaucer spoke of the conscientious pastor in 1387:

> Wide was his parish, with houses far asunder.
> But he never failed, for rain or thunder,
> In sickness or distress, to visit
> The furthest in his parish, high or low,
> Upon his feet – and in his hand a staff.

It is a touching scene, and the pastor trying 'to feed and provide for the Lord's family; to seek for Christ's sheep that are dispersed abroad, and for his children who are in the midst of this naughty world, that they may be saved through Christ for ever',[18] has a well-understood and honoured role in history.

The need for pastoral care is even greater in the modern world. The increase in divorce and unemployment, the turbulent pace of change and changing political attitudes, all leave in their wake an increasing and demanding army of the 'walking wounded', those who cannot cope and who have emotional and personal needs which cannot be met within the normal medical services and family context. Indeed the Christian church should be a haven for such folk, for a church should be a place of love. These are the people who pack the doctor's surgery seeking reassurance and getting pills, who crowd every social agency from the Samaritans to the Citizens' Advice Bureaux. Inevitably the church will be a lighthouse beckoning such people to the love of Christ expressed in the people of God. They are looking for an answer to those basic human and spiritual needs which we examined in Chapter 1. Indeed I find that a good indicator of the reality of love in a church is the proportion of such people in the congregation. If everyone is competent, well-adjusted, pleasant and undemanding, it suggests there is little love, or the 'walking wounded' would have been more in evidence, for every social group has many. It is likely that the national position is not going to change, except for the worse. To take only one example; it has been found that the children of divorced parents are three times more likely to be divorced themselves: what will the next generation be like?

All this calls into question the correct provision of pastoral care in the church by the leader or leaders. Certain questions need to be asked:

(1) *Is the pastor called to be a shepherd of the whole flock or primarily to be concerned with the individual?* Once again care is needed in dealing with the biblical images. The idea of the shepherd leaving the 99 in the wilderness and going in search of the individual 'until he finds it', is so powerful that we tend to think that the duty of the shepherd is primarily to look after the individual: this is reinforced by the individualism of much western thinking. But the overwhelming balance of the whole Bible is to see the shepherd as being particularly concerned

with the corporate, the flock rather than the individual sheep. In many Old Testament passages the 'shepherd' is the king of the nation who cared for the whole. In the New Testament, apart from the parable of the lost sheep, every other passage speaks of the shepherd looking after the flock; and in many the prevailing idea is of the shepherd sacrificing himself to carry out the task:

> The good shepherd lays down his life for the sheep. (John 10:11)

> Be shepherds of the church of God, which he brought with his own blood . . . savage wolves will come among you. (Acts 20:27)

> Be shepherds of God's flock that is under your care . . . eager to serve . . . being examples to the flock. (1 Pet. 5:2)

It is seen as a high calling that demands much.

(2) *Who should we pastor?* We can answer this too easily, by saying 'we must pastor those who are most in need'. But this can too soon become a matter of giving most pastoral care to those who demand it most frequently and most insistently. Should our care be demand-led in this way? One church, with a staff of four, wrote down at a staff meeting the people with whom they had had a time of real pastoral counselling during the previous week. There were 22 names on the list. A week later they repeated the exercise. There were now 24 names, including all the 22 of the week before. The pastoral care which four people could give was being sucked up by just over 20 people, while the other 200 or more in the congregation were being starved, let alone those who were not church members. The solution they came to was to ask each of the 'walking wounded' to accept a discipline, by which they had one member of staff at their entire disposal every four or five weeks for one and a half hours. Apart from this there were to be no phone calls late at night, no buttonholing after church services, no demands at any other times except in extreme emergency. After the inevitable uproar it was found that the workload of the staff in relation to these people lightened greatly, enabling them to care for others who were not clamouring for attention.

Further it was found that most of the people concerned, being forced to stand on their own feet, improved considerably. A friend of mine who was being submerged by demands asked a friendly psychiatrist what he should do. The reply was, 'professionalise it'. For many ministers who see themselves as available at all times it may be hard, but it may be a necessary shield against having a purely reactive ministry.

Dealing with individuals who present the most apparently pressing needs should not be the whole work of the pastor. He or she must remember that the flock is the real object of their care and sacrifice. Usually it is found that most of the work of the church is being done by a comparatively small body of people. They too need ongoing pastoral support. They may well not ask for it. Ministers too easily overlook their needs: 'Managers, being problem solvers, get sucked into the trap of reinforcing squeaking joints by paying attention to them and helping to solve their problems. All of which leaves little time to devote to the better producers who end up feeling neglected.'[19] It may be comforting for ministers to realise that business people get caught up in the same dilemma. We should be seeking to spend at least as much time with those who are vital for the running and mission of the church as we are with the 'squeaking joints'.

(3) *How far should a leader allow himself to be seen as a father-figure?* Any shepherd is liable to be regarded by the recipients of his care as the father-figure who can solve anything. He becomes the recipient of positive feelings in the same way as the *doulos*-slave receives negative emotions. Some clergy positively invite such a position by the use of the term 'Father', or by adopting an attitude of omnicompetence. It is a status which must be treated with great caution.

The 'hireling shepherd' of John 10 is distinguished from the 'good shepherd' because he fled when danger threatened. The followers of the shepherd look to him for commitment to them and their needs, particularly in the time of crisis. It is fatal for a shepherd to lack this care and concern for the flock. The biblical name for it is 'love'. A management consultant says, 'You get loyalty and commitment from people by giving it to them.'[20] St John of the Cross said the same long ago: 'Where there is no love, put love, and you will find love.' The position of a shepherd has to be earned. It is not one which is automatically given to a person by virtue of their leadership of a church.

This leads to a high degree of identification. The shepherd becomes the exemplar to the flock. He or she becomes the source of beliefs, values and standards of behaviour. In some ways this is good, and is a way to train others, but there is always the danger that the personality of others becomes submerged under the stronger personality of the leader. They merely copy blindly all his actions and thoughts, until these become unchallengeable. The results return to haunt his successor – 'The Revd X never did it like that.'

The danger is always present in this relationship that the person being cared for becomes over-dependent and shuffles off responsibility for their own life. Transference[21] may be necessary at certain times when a person is going through a crisis, but as a permanent relationship it is disastrous for both parties concerned. Further the shepherd can unwittingly become a God-figure and remove the necessity of personal reliance upon the Lord. This can also happen in the corporate setting, where a church becomes totally dependent upon a certain leader, seeing his word as the Word of God and his likes and dislikes as the way of the Spirit. It is sad when a leader leaves behind him a trail of people and churches which cannot manage without him.[22]

The Bible sees the shepherd as the one in the exposed place. At danger to himself he defends the flock from the encircling darkness and the beasts that prowl. That is part of the shepherd's work. But the shepherd is most at risk from the darkness within, where lie the wolves of self-deceit, self-aggrandisement and self-importance. Power intoxicates, especially power over people. 'Someone on a pedestal is easily knocked off.' The shepherd is particularly vulnerable to these temptations. They are warm feelings which make it all too easy to imagine we are helping people when all we are doing is binding them to ourselves and not directing them to God and personal responsibility for their own life.

The shepherd leads the flock to different places for pasture and rest. He is never prepared to leave them standing still in a cosy 1,9 position. Peter Drucker says 'a manager develops people', and so should the shepherd. Each member of the flock ought to be growing – as human beings as well as Christians – and it is our work to see that this is happening. Spiritual direction will be part of our work, seen not only in the narrow sense of developing the life of prayer, but maturing the whole person.[23] Part of this process will be leading each person into an adult relationship with those who have authority over them in the church, in their family and at work.

Steward

A 'steward'[24] had to be responsible to his master for the care of his property. Although it might be a servile job carried out by slaves, it could also be work carried out by an important person with wide responsibilities: Erastus is described in Romans 16:23 as 'the *oikonomos* of the city' and may have been the man who was influential enough to have his name inscribed on the tablet which was unearthed at Corinth in 1929.

The steward is the central figure in a number of parables and stories told by Christ. They show the characteristics looked for in a good steward: faithfulness and loyalty, business acumen (even a willingness to engage in sharp practice), and the ability to discipline and care for those under him. He had to have a sense of responsibility when the master was absent for he was above all someone who was accountable to his superior for what he did.

Christian leaders are described as 'stewards of the mysteries of God' (1 Cor. 4:1). The title is given specifically to the *episkopos* in Titus 1:7, and it is used more widely to describe the nature of Christian ministry in other passages.[25]

Each of the three main requirements of a good steward is an important feature of good leadership.

First he is *accountable to God for his people*. When a minister talks about 'my' church it can be either a good sign or a bad one. It may be that he is identifying with the congregation, so that there is no sense of 'me' and 'them'; but the word may be used in the sense of ownership. If this is so then he is being a poor steward, for he forgets who is the Master of the church and to whom he is accountable. I find that one of the most uncomfortable questions it is possible to ask a minister and his or her congregation is, 'who is in charge here?'

Secondly *he is responsible to the church for the past*. He must value the tradition which has come from the past, and take from its treasure chest those things which are valuable, while discarding the impedimenta.

Thirdly *he is responsible to the church for the future*. He must keep before people the vision of what is yet to be attained, 'until the Master returns'.

Tradition can be valuable or otherwise. Every church has a history. There are the great 'mysteries' of which the New Testament speaks and which come to us from the apostolic past and are enshrined in the Bible and the creeds. There is the denominational past which governs much of the ethos of any church. Finally there is the particular story of the local church. Each of these elements add up to make a formidable weight of tradition. Much of it is indispensable, much of it is useful, but some of it clogs the wheels. There is a real need to distinguish between tradition and traditionalism. The former is the sound core of faith and practice which has been handed down to us. The latter is that part of the past which people mistake for the truth, and which has become an idol deflecting them from the worship of the true God. 'Tradition is the living faith of the dead; traditionalism is the dead faith of the living.'

It has to be noted that there is often a wide divergence between a congregation's perception of tradition and what is true. They frequently have a view of the past, or of what is imagined to be the tradition of their denomination, which is very different from reality. Churches have 'folk memories'. The most common is of some far off 'golden days' when the church was full and 'we were one big happy family'. The registers and other documents in the church may tell a very different story but the congregation finds it difficult to come to terms with what it was actually like in the past. When tradition is being encountered it is the *perceived* rather than the *actual* tradition which has to be taken into account. In this context myths are more important than history. For example, many Methodists see abstinence from alcohol as part of their title deeds, but in fact it was an outcome of the Temperance Movement of the 1820s and 1830s. The general belief has to be accepted as fact, even if it be mistaken.

The work of the steward is to sift through the tradition, to distinguish that which throbs with continued life from that which has no further value, and to pass its riches on to the new generation. It is a mistake to believe that we have no further use for the past. An age which thinks little of history is an age without roots, and a church which despises the past will have no springboard from which to vault into the future. Christian history has shown time and again that it is wrong and impossible to abolish tradition.

But the steward is not only to look after what the Master gives us from the past, but to cherish what is given by the Master for the future. Josephine Bax describes ministers as being 'keepers of the vision'.[26] It is part of the leader's task to make sure that he or she knows what the will of God is and to keep it steadily in front of the people in the church. The vision is a 'statement of purpose' which defines the focus of the church, but it is much more than that – it has to have the touch of the Holy Spirit about it. It must capture the imagination as well as the minds of the congregation, and give direction to everything the church does.

So important is the establishing, nurture and implementation of the vision that Chapter 5 is given to this. Just as a manager has to keep before the workforce the goals of the firm so a Christian minister needs to make sure:

(1) that there is a vision to set before people;

(2) that it is a vision from God, rather than a personal whim or a compromise between conflicting political forces;

(3) that the vision is developed as time passes (more detail is filled in, new areas come into view as parts of it are fulfilled);

(4) that the vision beams steadily not fitfully;

(5) that the vision is accepted as right by a large majority of the people in the church.

If he or she is to be the 'keeper of the vision' then *the leader must also be a planner*. It may be the work of a prophet to set out some part of a vision, but it requires a planner to make sure that the steps which lead to the attainment of the vision are followed. The leader has to 'earth' the majesty of the vision, show the path towards it, ensure that something happens. Otherwise the vision will fade, the people become frustrated, and the church will return to a 5,5 position of mutual bickering.

Episkopos

One minister I knew was a wonderful shepherd of the individuals in his congregation: he served them day and night at great personal cost. He was a faithful steward of the Word of God. But he was not an *episkopos* and he did not allow anyone else to fulfil this role. As a result his church was rudderless and uncoordinated. Little groups of people undertook conflicting projects without communicating with each other; there was no overall budgetry control of money and other resources; there was a lack of oversight and discipline. The result was a frustrated, diminishing congregation which almost fell apart when he died.

Some would link this function in Scripture with that of the apostle. Whatever our view of this may be, the need for such a coordinating function in the church is obvious. Certainly its lack is all too unmistakable. The pace of change and movement within both church and society means that a church without guidance of this sort is a storm-tossed ship without a captain.

The word *episkopos* can be translated 'bishop' (as in the Authorised Version) and is enshrined in such words as 'episcopal'. We must rid our minds of such connotations. The word *skopos* means 'watcher'. Hence an *epi-skopos* is 'someone who watches over'. The rather old-fashioned word 'overseer' describes it exactly, for it implies a broad perspective and a care for all.

An *episkopos* can only operate within the overall *episkope* of the whole Body of Christ. It is for this reason that ordination in most denominations involves those from outside the local situation. It is remarkable that in the three Pauline passages which set out the different ministries in the church (Rom. 12; 1 Cor. 12; Eph. 4) the imagery of the Body is employed in each instance as the setting in which these 'love gifts' of God to the church are mounted. There is no place for self-appointed freelance ministries, and they should be looked upon with considerable reserve.

There are other words which cluster around this idea. *Proistemi* describes the work of the 'manager', someone put in charge of others and responsible for them: it is used several times in 1 Timothy 3:4–12 to describe the control that elders and deacons should have over their families. *Kubernesis* can be translated 'administration', but the root meaning is that of the 'helmsman' who steers the ship. The wind of the Holy Spirit blows and drives the ship along, but it is the steersman who guides it safely into port. [27]

One word which is identical to *episkopos* is *presbuteros*, usually translated 'elder'. It has been shown long since[28] that the two words are used interchangeably in the New Testament, and that it was only in post-apostolic times that the *episkopos* could be identified as someone who presided over the presbyters.

There is one title used in the New Testament to describe leadership that is *never* used of the Christian minister. There are 109 occurrences of the words which stem from *archon*, 'a ruler'. They are used frequently of secular authorities; they are used of the 'principalities and powers' (*archais kai exousiais*);

one of them (*archegos*) is even used several times as a description of Christ himself; but never are they used to describe a Christian leader. On the plinth of a memorial in Southwell Minster to a great bishop three words are inscribed, 'Scholar . . . Pastor . . . Ruler'. The last is not a correct description for a Christian. The 'rulers of the Gentiles' may be called such, but for the Christian there can be only one ruler, who is the *archegos tes zoes*, the Prince of Life.[29] It is a useful reminder that no one in Christian leadership should ever rule another person. Whenever this has happened there has been disaster, for the authority given by the Spirit has been exercised as though it were the authority of this world and it both demeans the person who seeks to control and dethrones the true Ruler. 'The free man has never been a religious tyrant, nor has he lorded it over God's heritage. It is fear and lack of self-assurance that has led men to try to crush others under their feet.'[30]

> Be shepherds of God's flock that is under your care, serving as overseers – not because you must, but because you are willing, as God wants you to be; not greedy for money, but eager to serve; not lording it over those entrusted to you, but being examples to the flock. (1 Pet. 5:2,3)

The four main functions of the *episkopos* are extremely important:

(1) The prime task is *oversight*. The *episkopos* must be aware of events and care continually for those for whom he or she is responsible. In the hands of an *episkopos* who is unsure of himself this can become a ministry of prying, seeking to know everything about everybody. That is not true oversight. There are times when great areas of work need to be given over to others, and they should be left to get on with it without interference; for to interfere shows a lack of trust, both in the people concerned and in one's own judgement in delegating the task to those people in the first place. There are other times when supervision needs to be close and constant, especially

when a new project is being set up or difficulties have been encountered. Oversight without love can be harsh and over-bearing, but with love it is welcomed and respected. This is shown most clearly in the *episkopos* as a person of prayer. Because he is the only peron who knows the overall picture only he can pray with real knowledge. To fail in this means that the church is defenceless. The New Testament epistles are full of oversight. Even though written from many miles away, and sometimes from a prison cell, they all reveal a close concern for and knowledge of the local situation and give advice and help, with the assurance of constant prayer.

(2) Oversight will inevitably result in the *episkopos* being a *coordinator of the work of others*. He or she must seek to bring everything in the church into the service of the vision which has been given. There must be a recognition that God has given gifts to his church, and that these gifts are *people*: each has its own ministry and has to be dovetailed into the ministries of others. If this does not happen the prophet will prophesy and no one will integrate his insights into the whole; the teacher will teach, but his teaching will not fit any coherent pattern; the pastor will care but with no framework in which to do so. We get glimpses of this in the New Testament when Peter and Paul in their different epistles tell each group of people – children, parents, slaves, elders etc. – to get on with their ministry. Without coordination there is a great waste of time, much uncertainty among those who are led, and a lack of any sense of direction.

(3) Inevitably because of the nature of oversight there will have to be a degree of *discipline* in the work of the *episkopos*. This can be seen as purely negative. But a good parent does not discipline a child only with punishments. There is the greater discipline of love. The Pauline commands vary from 'consigning to Satan' to 'appeal to the older man as though he were your father'. There is much unease in the modern church about this. There have been painful cases in the past where corrective discipline has been exercised in a way which has been harsh

and destructive. There have been situations where the focus
has been almost entirely upon a select number of sins – usually
the most publicly obvious – as though these were the only faults
that count. Greed, selfishness and pride have gone unrebuked
while there has been much head-shaking over improper sexual
relationships and drunkenness. But the need for discipline in
the church should not be avoided because it has been
mishandled. Abuses arise when the biblical pattern is forgotten,
a pattern which in the New Testament concentrates on the
reconciliation of the sinner to God. 'Neither the purity of the
church nor the restoration of sinners to the church are ends in
themselves. They are milestones on the way to the ultimate
goal of ending our alienation from God and each other. Putting
reconciliation first and letting it rule over the other aims of
corrective discipline will protect us from using it cruelly.'[31] The
biblical commands are surprisingly specific:

(a) If sin which requires action by the leadership is suspected,
    begin by talking it over privately: 'go and show him his
    fault, just between the two of you'. [32] The need for confid-
    entiality which the passage enjoins is important. As a leader
    it is easier to indulge in 'pious gossip' by talking over
    someone's faults with other leaders than to discuss it face
    to face with the person concerned. So often one has only
    a partial view of the situation, and explanations are all
    that is required to show the area of misunderstanding.
    Therefore the approach by the leader should be that of a
    Christian friend seeking to resolve a difficulty, rather than
    the condemnatory accusation which a degree of nervous-
    ness (on either side) may engender. If the sin is real enough
    then the fact of it being known by another will often lead
    to repentance and reconciliation, and 'you have won your
    brother over'. Unfortunately leaders too often avoid the
    possibility of embarrassing confrontation and hope that
    procrastination will make the problem disappear. The
    result is that the sin eats into the church like a cancer.
    The reason why Paul urged Euodia and Syntyche to be

reconciled to each other was because their quarrel imperilled the whole church at Philippi.

(b) Only if this personal approach fails should there be a more formal approach. Beforehand the leader needs to examine his own motives: is there any personal rancour . . . Pharisaism . . . cruelty . . . lust for domination? This is particularly important when the person concerned is of the opposite sex, for unacknowledged motivations are more common in such cases. After this it is necessary to go to the person concerned with 'one or two others' [33] and it is wise if one of them is of the opposite sex to oneself. Once again you go in love as a reconciler rather than an accuser, seeking to bring the person to be reconciled with God and others. There may need to be more than one meeting. There is a tendency for the person initially to bluster and deny the truth out of embarrassment rather than obduracy, and further meetings may enable this to be faced. Time and prayer will give an opportunity for him to face up to reality.

(c) It is only after this has failed that there should be an open discussion about the situation within the church at large. 'Tell it to the church.'[34] Here too the leader should seek to show the greatest possible love to the person concerned. Where this ministry has been misused it has been because there has been the atmosphere of a kangaroo court rather than that of Christians coming as sinners to reconcile a fellow-sinner. Above all every effort should be made to avoid the creation of factions which support or condemn the person involved: the church should see itself as coming together to find the way of God in a difficult situation.

There are few tasks which require a Christian leader to have a finer sensitivity, a more precise sense of timing, and a greater need to walk with God. Discipline should not come easily to us; if it does we should have nothing to do with it for it is feeding something unwholesome within ourselves.

(4) Every organisation needs a focal point, and this is often

concentrated on one person or a small group of people. The *episkopos* is the 'persona' who is seen *by the outside world* as the church's representative and its spokesperson on matters concerning the church. When Stewart examined the work that managers actually did, she found that the most common style was that of the 'emissary': those who spent much time with people other than their own employees.[35] Inevitably the minister is seen by the outside world as fulfilling this role, hence the invitation to sit on the platform, join that committee, and 'say a few words' on each occasion. It is easy to feel that this role is useless window-dressing, but used thoughtfully it can be a valuable opportunity for Christian witness. Inevitably it is usually 'presence' rather than 'proclamation' evangelism, but the one can lead to the other. This 'networking' can bear fruit in many unexpected ways.

For the minister this can be dangerous ground. To be asked for an opinion by the media and to be honoured as a person representing an important element within society can lead to being given the 'chief seats', and it is important to realise that we are in such symbolic positions only because of Christ and his church, and that we represent them best by humility and a readiness to speak for him in public places, rather than by being drawn unthinkingly into the personal infighting, political stances and status seeking of others. The opposite danger is of an undemanding blandness, where we bestow a Cheshire Cat-like grin on all we survey. The minister is not to be an amiable and harmless relic of the past giving a benign blessing on everything, but a light to the world and a standard of truth.

The behaviour of the leader

We have looked at the different roles that the New Testament gives to the leader. It has almost as much material on the personal requirements of the leader. Just as 1 Corinthians 13 says that any charism exercised without love is empty and self-defeating, so the charism of leadership without love is empty and even dangerous. Several passages set out the 'personal specification'[36] for those who are to be chosen as leader.

Five requirements for a leader appear in these lists:[37]

(1) The person must have a good reputation outside as well as inside the church. A good leader is respected and has 'weight' in the community. Without that he or she will speak and no one will listen, and they will lead but no one will follow. This is more than merely being well spoken of, it is a matter of trust. Reputation comes from a trust in the person; hence the shock which occurs when a doctor or lawyer or priest abuses the faith which is placed in them.

(2) A leader must have a family life above reproach, for 'if anyone does not know how to manage his own family, how can he take care of God's church?' It is remarkable that the personal character of the marriage partner and children have to be taken into account: this is contrary to modern views which wish to see spouses and children as separate entities, and do not wish to appear to penalise one for the shortcomings of another. Experience suggests that the modern view is wrong, particularly where the marriage partner is concerned. A family is a unit and members of it cannot be fully judged except in that context. The ministry of a leader is inevitably going to be helped or hindered by their family. One bishop remarked, 'The ministry of half my clergy is made by their wives, and the other half have it destroyed by them.'

(3) Their personal life should be honest. The danger of love of money is mentioned in particular, as though this was a difficulty which the early church faced frequently.

(4) They should be kind, hospitable and gentle, not quick-tempered or drunken (again, the frequency with which this is mentioned suggests that it may have been a common problem).

(5) They should have spiritual maturity, and a strong grasp of the Gospel.

There is one word which encompasses all the above, and which is much used by writers on modern management: *integrity*. The word implies unity of life and consistency of action. 'Subordinates may forgive a great deal: incompetence, ignorance, insecurity or bad manners. But they will never forgive a lack of integrity. Nor will they forgive higher management for choosing such a person.' These words of Peter Drucker are frequently echoed by other writers, so important is it seen to be. It is significant that both etymologically and in practice the word integrity is allied with the word 'holiness'.

A minister has to steer his or her way through many mazes. There is a great deal to be said for keeping everything at one's fingertips, monitoring and checking all that is going on. There is even more to be said for delegating, letting go, trusting others to get on with the job. There is much to be said for acting as a mission agency of the church, working primarily on the frontier. There is also much to be said for spending time with members of the congregation so that they are the missionaries. Leadership involves handling opposites and the art of compromise. If we have no personal integrity then we merely take the soft option, or listen to the loudest voice, and people become uncertain as to where they stand. If we have unclear personal values and uncertain goals then we cannot expect other people to follow us freely. The disciples followed Christ 'gladly' because of his wholeness of being and his clear personal vision.

More than most people, leaders need to love themselves in the way that Christ taught, 'love your neighbour *as yourself*'. Those who have a right regard for themselves and their ministry are able to be outgoing and relaxed, and this in turn builds trust and confidence in others. One cannot love oneself in this way unless you are confident of the love of God for yourself. 'We love because he first loved us.'

This implies an emotional freedom which may be difficult for those in northern latitudes to attain.[38] There is a passion about the Christian faith which requires an emotional investment difficult for some. But if leaders are personally cold and aloof, it is not surprising that they preach a Christianity which is uninteresting, uninspiring and unchallenging. One of the results of the recent work of the Holy Spirit, principally through the charismatic movement, has been the emotional freeing and healing of many ministers. If, with Bishop Butler in the eighteenth century, we see enthusiasm as 'a very horrid thing', then it is unlikely that we shall be able to enthuse and motivate others. A salesman is taught to believe in his product and commit himself to it. The Christian Gospel does not need selling like soap powder, but there must be a total commitment to it with every fibre of our being, which means the emotions as well as the intellect, the heart as well as the mind.

The marks of a leader without this self-confidence and integrity will be all too obvious:

(1) In order to bolster his own confidence he belittles other people, like a child stamping on the sand castles of other youngsters so that his own may be the tallest. He concentrates on others' weaknesses rather than their strengths. He denigrates their achievements. There is a need for the large-heartedness of Paul who could say 'I have great confidence in you; I take great pride in you. I am greatly encouraged'.[39] This sign of insecurity has serious manifestations. In particular it can lead to cynicism. To see the world with a sneer is the complete opposite of Christ, who sees the truth yet loves despite it.

(2) Such leaders will appear 'twitchy' and uncertain in personal relationships. Colin Urquhart tells how people in his church used to say to him, 'Colin, we do not know you,' and how he would say to himself, 'Good.' But if we are not prepared to be vulnerable and open to people, then it is not likely that they will be open about themselves and we shall not be given the privilege of pastoring them. One minister I knew was a splendid counsellor, well-trained and sensitive. But because he could only operate within a professional, client-counsellor relationship, hardly anybody came to him for ministry because they did not know him well enough to trust. We build a wall of protection and hide behind it from the real or pretended attacks

of others. It may be more comfortable, but we are not following the One who was prepared to be vulnerable to all, even his enemies.

(3) Creativity comes from a secure base, and a willingness to expend energy. Energy is finite, like a certain sum of money. If we spend too much on inner heart-searching, we shall only have small change left to spend on solving problems and seeking vision for the church. Further we shall not be able to accept the creative insights of others if we are overconcerned with ourselves. If, when discussing a problem, we find ourselves saying 'Who is right?' rather than 'What is right?' we betray a lack of integrity.

(4) Inner absorption often makes us unaware of the effect we have upon others. It is a salutary exercise to ask people to say frankly how we appear to them. We may be quite unaware that we are evoking reactions such as fear, distrust, envy or even hatred. It is particularly difficult for those who see themselves essentially as reconcilers to cope with the fact that they are not universally liked and trusted. But discovering these views, accepting them and handing them over to God is a necessary sign of maturity. It should be stressed that these are reactions to us as a person, not just to us as ministers in the servant role which means that we are recipients of negative feelings. The world heaped hatred and rejection on Christ and he told us it would come our way: 'Woe is you when all men speak well of you.' But we need to check that any rejection of us is due to the Gospel we minister rather than the person we are. It is too easy for us to avoid the pain of personal rejection by pretending it is the Gospel.

Integrity of behaviour and the resulting self-confidence will enable us to be more aware of the world around us. If we are conscious of our need in this area – and many Christian leaders have a low self-image – then we must seek for healing and encouragement from others. It is paradoxical that to forget ourselves we have to know ourselves. We need to 'own' our emotions, come to a clearer view of ourselves as human beings, pray for insights into our inner motivations and convictions. We do this, not in order that we might be happier or nicer people (for to do that is to seek to save our own life, and in doing so to lose it). Rather we do it for the sake of those whom God has called us to serve. Christ prayed: 'For their sakes I consecrate myself.'[40] It should be our prayer also.

Conclusion

In this chapter we have examined some of the biblical material relating to leadership, centering it around the four roles of scriptural leadership: servant, shepherd, steward and *episkopos*. It is important for any leader to evaluate himself or herself in relation to these four areas of ministry. Preferably get someone else, who knows you well, to do it with you.

How do you rate on a scale of 1 to 10 in each field? If necessary reread the appropriate parts of the chapter to refresh your memory. Jot down your results as a bar chart (e.g. Fig. 5).

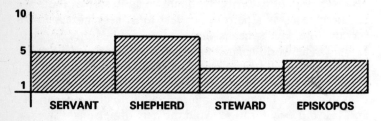

Fig. 5

You will notice that the person evaluated has a bias towards the left-hand side: he is better at caring for the individual than the corporate. He will need to make sure that the latter does not get neglected because he is likely to enjoy being a carer and encourager of people.

Every church is entitled to 10 . . . 10 . . . 10 . . . 10 leadership and it is likely that God has provided for this. What about the unshaded area above your personal level on the graph? This area represents the leadership which is *not* being provided by yourself. Part of your work as leader will be to look at the church and discover those people who can make up what you lack. A church should be led by a team rather than by an individual. No one person can be a 10 . . . 10 . . . 10 . . . 10 leader: it is likely that very few can really provide a 10 point leadership in any of the four roles. What you cannot do others need to do. But these people are not merely called in to make up your shortcomings. They have their own charism of leadership from God. If they are unable to exercise it they will be frustrated and the true work of God through their lives will run into the sand.

To discover, train and use the leadership gifts of others is one of the most worthwhile and satisfying tasks of a leader. At times it may be a matter of 'he must increase, and I must decrease' as we get out of the way to enable others to grow, but to see someone you have known and nurtured begin to blossom into ministry gives a thrill that little else can surpass. To remember that this person, now leading with confidence and wisdom, was a few years ago shy and unhappy, is fulfilment indeed. Paul expressed it: 'I always pray with joy because of your partnership in the gospel from the first day until now, being confident of this, that he who began a good work in you will carry it on to completion until the day of Christ Jesus.'[41]

3

The Team

The end of Chapter 1 introduced the idea of the 'flower-pot' church, where the leadership sought to enable the ministries of the members of the congregation. It was pointed out that 'turning the flower pot upside down' was very often the result of a process of renewal in the church which had lasted for a period of years.[1]

In Chapter 2 the impossibility of one person providing a full 10 . . . 10 . . . 10 . . . 10 scriptural pattern of leadership was spelt out. The tasks are too numerous, and the skills required too varied, for one person. Even if some Atlas could carry the whole church on his shoulders, it would be to its ultimate detriment. Indeed it is often part of the process of 'turning upside down' that there is the recognition of the need for a team of people to undertake leadership. Unfortunately the team can be set up in an inappropriate way, with little regard to the future and without answering some of the basic questions which need to be asked. It has to be admitted that the failure rate of 'teams', particularly those which have been formalised as 'elderships', has been high. Many churches would echo the experience of business consultants: 'A team has the potential to accomplish much more than the sum of its individual members. However groups often fail to achieve even a small fraction of their potential . . . it is not a universal panacea for all management problems.'[2]

The importance of teams

It is useless to embark on setting up a team in the church unless *the church members*, as well as the leader, are convinced of its rightness. Teams have been introduced because the leader has read a book or visited another church and then imposed the concept on a congregation whose view can best be described as bewildered suspicion. The idea must be introduced with great care and widespread consultation (especially as one is disturbing that most precious of patterns in a human organisation, the balance of power). A congregation has not only to be taught about the rightness of teams. Wherever possible, it needs to have a 'working example' demonstrated in a church which is not too dissimilar to itself. A visit to or from such an exemplar may do more than any number of sermons or teaching sessions.

Moreover it is not sufficient merely to show that team leadership is scriptural or even sensible, if the hidden questions are not addressed. Every member of the congregation naturally asks 'where does this leave me?' and that question has to be answered to the reasonable satisfaction of the church members if the team is to have a chance of acceptance by the congregation.

Church members look to the leadership for four needs:

Decision-making. They need to know a clearly defined route by which decisions are reached. This means an openness about the process. If the introduction of a team suggests that decisions will now be made by a semi-secret body there will be difficulties, especially if one of the existing power structures feels that power is being taken out of their hands. This will be even more acute if people feel that they are held to be responsible for decisions in which they had no hand. An Anglican PCC member of long-standing grumbled, '*They* make all the decisions and people complain to *us*.'

Direction. People will be used to church policy being enunciated by one person. If this becomes a group pronouncement the trumpet may have an uncertain sound, because the message may lack precision. Further the congregation looks for accountability and information: 'Who are we to go to to find out more (and who are we to blame for it)?'

Dependency needs. Everyone likes to have one person to refer to at a time of crisis. People do not like teams of doctors or lawyers where there may be no known or identifiable face. We do not like it any more in the church, which should above all seek to care for the individual and affirm his or her worth. Does the introduction of the team mean that people do not know whom to turn to?

Development. The church should be the place where people enter through the work of the Holy Spirit into a greater maturity. They find themselves becoming capable of things they never thought possible. To be aware of how God is seeking to mature each person and to help the process forward is time-consuming and demanding. One person cannot do it in a congregation of any size, and a team becomes imperative. The same pattern is happening in industry, and for the same reason. Charles Handy writes: 'Times are changing in some organisations, where the idea of the president's office, a triumvirate or quadumvirate of top talent acting as a team, is becoming more frequent, as an adaptive recognition that the prime task of the directorate is one of development, not of personal intervention.'[3] For this reason any team that is established must not stifle the congregation but rather enable each individual to grow to their full potential as members of a flower-pot church.

Each of these 'Four-Ds' has to be taken into account when setting up a team. Despite all the caveats which must rightly be spelt out, the usefulness of teams is clear. The reasons can be set out under five headings:

(1) *Scripture*. Whether we look at the initial missionary efforts, the founding of churches or the continuation of churches which have been in existence for 20 years or more, we find the team is normal. The Jewish converts were used to the traditional

pattern of 'the elders of the synagogue' and found no difficulty in transferring the idea into the early church. Paul formed teams of elders in newly established churches and told Titus to do the same.[4]

(2) *Common sense*. For the reasons described in the first two chapters it is unreasonable to expect one person to have all the gifts of leadership. Congregations can come to realise this. They will also be pleased that decisions tend to be slower, partly because there is a need to refer them to the team, and partly because a team may not make up its collective mind as smartly as an individual. Church members do not like their church being run by one person's passing enthusiasms, and can come to recognise that a team leads to 'rounder', more considered decisions.

(3) *Strategy*. One of the earliest and most valuable findings of the Church Growth school[5] is that a church will cease to grow when the numbers within it get to about 175 because the leader is at full stretch and the congregation settles into a 'steady state' position, i.e. where the number of newcomers is balanced by those who leave. Team leadership gives the opportunity to grow through this barrier. A team is able 'to ensure that an appropriate ministry of Word and Sacraments is provided'.[6]

(4) *Charismata*. Almost certainly God has given the charism of leadership to more than one person in the congregation, and if these charismata are not used, the people concerned will be discontented and unfulfilled. They are the people who suggest ways forward, think widely, and at worst are centres of disaffection. Many splinter churches have been formed by someone with a charism of leadership which is not affirmed and used within the parent church. He or she leads a group of people into a new fellowship. In such cases the blame for the sin of schism is not only to be laid on the shoulders of the person who led the breakaway, but also on the church leadership which failed to recognise a charism.

(5) *Support*. There are two areas where support is needed.

First, the minister and other leaders have their personal needs and these must be ministered to. However it has to be spelt out that a leadership team is not primarily a support for personal needs. Its work is to look outwards in caring for the church and community, and upwards to the Lord. But there is another area needing support. Decisions should be checked, and guidance must be validated before being accepted as God-given. A team can perform this function well when fellow-leaders gather to pray and discuss. The joint decisions which result are more balanced than if they are subject to the enthusiasms and interests of an individual. Further it means that the person who is implementing the decision has a greater confidence in its rightness when it has been talked through and decided upon by the team.

The questions which need to be asked and answered

A leadership team is intended to be a foundation stone for the church. It should therefore not be laid without much thought and prayer. Some schemes have been founded on sand, and have tumbled as soon as difficulties have arisen. Some churches which have successfully introduced teams would say that it takes five years before the team is accepted by the congregation as part of the landscape. It is therefore worthwhile spending time founding the team on rock.

(1) *What is the relation between the 'normal' structures of church life and the leadership team?* Much depends on the way in which the team comes into being. Many churches have found to their surprise that a team has evolved without a conscious policy decision. There are three common ways in which this can happen:

(a) house group leaders have met frequently with the church leaders to prepare the programme for future group sessions: it is not a long step from discussing the teaching

which needs to be given to thinking through the future
direction of the whole church;

(b) the minister gathers an *ad hoc* group to discuss the problems and opportunities in the church. This 'sounding
board' becomes increasingly conscious of its unity and
cohesiveness and begins to turn almost imperceptibly into
a leadership team. In many ways this form of evolution is
an excellent way to begin: it is an organic growth from
within the existing situation rather than an alien implant,
and it enables the charisms of others to be discovered.
Nevertheless there should come a time when a group which
has evolved in this way recognises what has happened and
adjusts its behaviour accordingly;

(c) more managerial in tone and more common in large
churches, the 'heads of departments' gather to discuss their
mutual concerns and plan policy.

At other times there is already a group of leaders. This may
be demanded by existing denominational structures (e.g. the
deacons of a Baptist church). It may be an official grouping
which has been operating for some time (e.g. a standing
committee) or it may be a powerful unofficial group of people
who have 'run the church'. Any suggestion of a 'leadership
team' will pose an immediate threat to their power. There are
likely to be many difficulties unless the existing group can be
changed into the new team. There have been many instances
where the work of the Holy Spirit has done just that, through
much prayer and patience. But it does not always happen!
Careful talking through with the members of the existing group
can be fruitful, and it may be that some of its members would
be good people in the new team. However, such a smooth
transition may not be possible and it may regretfully have to
be accepted that a straight conflict with the existing order may
not be right, however beneficial a team may be thought to be.
God may want other things from the church than a prolonged
period of disturbance concerning structure.

The other area to be considered is the existing committee

structure. Most denominations have some sort of church committee or parochial church council, and a number of church officers. But the amount of real power which resides in these bodies varies widely from church to church. Whatever the strict legal position may be, in some places committees are so used to the autocratic diktat of the minister or 'those who run the church' that they exercise little real power, and a new system is easily assimilated; they do not miss power that they never had. In other churches there is a very active and interested and powerful existing structure, which will vigorously oppose any interference.

There seems to be little value in taking power from bodies where it is being used responsibly in order to have an up-to-date or even apparently scriptural pattern. Team leadership should in these cases become part of what already exists, possibly operating as a standing committee of the main committee. One church which had had a team for some years recently merged it with the PCC because 'it had become the team itself'.

Where the existing committees are working badly but exercising much power – often blocking any new initiatives in the church – the situation is more difficult. As one Anglican priest in a Yorkshire parish was told quite frankly, 'We've seen out five vicars and we'll see out thee.' It is unlikely that there will be much support for the minister in these situations. It is especially important in these cases, if a team is established, for there to be a formal link between the existing structures and the team. Many churches have found that it is helpful if the team is designated a sub-committee of the church committee. This means that it reports to its parent body, and can use the committee as a sounding board for its ideas. This can overcome some of the suspicions which a team can generate in these difficult circumstances.

In most denominational structures the relationship of the team to the bishop, superintendent, etc. has to be taken into account. Their understanding and general acceptance is important, not least because in many denominations they have a say in the appointment of ministers. Some will readily recognise a team as a possible form of church life, and bishops etc. may be happy to come and commission a newly-formed team: the advantage of this for the acceptance of the team by the congregation as a whole cannot be underestimated. At other times the denominational authorities will have nothing to do with it, and prefer to work through the 'official' pattern. This seems to be particularly true of denominations like the United Reformed or Baptist churches which have an existing group leadership structure. Whatever attitude they adopt, the authorities need to know what is intended, if only because they may well have to cope if there are subsequent difficulties.

(2) *What is the relation between the congregation and the team?* Acceptance grows from real understanding. Prayer, communication and time are the three necessary ingredients to ensure that the team is accepted and used by church members. This means long consultations before the team is established and much explanation of why it is being done. It is particularly important to understand people's fears, for the negative forces have to be faced and talked through. If a team evolves it is easier than if it is introduced suddenly, but in either case much communication needs to take place. Sound buildings are not built overnight, and it may take many months before a team can be properly introduced. One Baptist church which has a successful pattern took over two years between the initial suggestion and its implementation. Jerry-built shacks soon fall down.

There is no doubt that the word 'elder' raises doubts in many people's minds. This is partly because 'elder' is the title of a church officer in some denominations – and 'we are not like them' – and partly because the word suggests a group of greybeards. There is no point in struggling about a word which inevitably does not have the same connotations now as it did in the days of the New Testament, and may be best avoided. Such descriptions as 'lay pastor', 'pastoral leader', 'member of the ministry team' have all been used. Although less scriptural and less succinct than the term 'elder' they are also less threatening.

If team leadership is foisted on a suspicious congregation then difficulties inevitably follow. The means by which the team is chosen will make a considerable difference to this. There are various models:

(a) in some churches the congregation is asked to suggest names and the final decision is made by the leader(s);
(b) in others, the names of prospective team members are chosen by the other leaders and put before the congregation for their vote at a properly convened church meeting;
(c) in others the congregation both proposes names and votes on them.

Most church leaders feel that some sort of safeguard is required to prevent unsuitable people being elected on to the team. They will need to work closely with any new person, to feel spiritually of a common mind, and to know that the one proposed has a deep commitment to the church. Hence (a) and (b) are probably the commonest methods of appointment. Whichever method is chosen the ordinary members of the church must have a say at some point. Often the PCC or other church committee is asked to ratify the choice made by the leadership team.

The congregation will be more welcoming to the team if it is seen not to be the 'vicar's clique', and has people who are prepared to put question marks against accepted policy. If names are suggested only by the existing leadership there is the danger of excluding people who have a real charism of leadership but who may be angular in personality or unorthodox in viewpoint. A team of clones is not beneficial to a church. God's saints are not usually conformists, and a true Christian leader is not a 'company man' who allows himself to be moulded by the environment. There needs to be a place for the maverick and the questioner, the lateral thinker and the dreamer. It is a sign of assured leadership to use well those who do not agree with you.[7]

When choosing new team members it may be important to realise that it is not always necessary for everyone to *like* the new person. Personal relationships are important in forwarding the work – they improve communication, speed decision-making and give a model of Christian fellowship – but a group of the like-minded is no model of the catholicity of the church. It is noticeable that some leadership teams have very uncertain personal relationships and yet the work of God goes steadily forward despite this. Conversely I have encountered teams who spend so much time working at their own relationships that they achieve little for the life of the church. After all Paul would have achieved less if he had had lengthy counselling to sort out his personal reaction to the quarrel with Barnabas about John Mark, or had spent long hours sitting on a committee in Jerusalem trying to resolve the differences in the relationships between the Gentiles and the Jews.

(3) *What is the relationship between the minister and the team?*
Many difficulties within a team are caused by members of the team having different expectations. If the minister sees the others as purely advisory, while they expect that agreements reached will be put into effect, there is a fruitful ground for discord. If one member sees himself as representing the interests of an organisation and the others see themselves as seeking to exercise *episkope* over the whole church there will be problems.[8]

It is important that all members have the same understanding of their task. Further, if (as often happens) the objectives or method of working of the team changes, then what is happening needs to be made clear to all members. There should be a regular review of the working of the team, not to indulge in inappropriate self-criticism but to recognise how God is working in the team and to set fresh goals and deepen the understanding of the dynamics of the group. Some teams have found it useful to use an outside consultant who can come in occasionally to help with this exercise: the third party can enable truths to be faced which would otherwise be hidden because of politeness, or an unwillingness 'to rock the boat'.

Three difficulties often occur:

(a) The minister or another person within the group does not exercise the charism of discernment. As a result there is no stabilising influence. Studies show that people working in groups tend to advocate more venturesome options than they would if they were making an individual decision about the same situation. This so-called 'risky-shift' can come about because individuals are not called upon to be personally accountable for team decisions, or because there is a group expectation of radical thinking. This can be disguised as taking a 'leap of faith'. This may of course be right, but group enthusiasm is not necessarily the same as the word of the Lord.

(b) The minister shuffles off responsibility, in effect saying to the team, 'You must make all the decisions, I am sitting back and praying for you.' This leaves the team without a chairman or a focus. Inevitably it will be the minister who is most likely to enunciate the policy to the congregation and who will receive any unease. He cannot abdicate. There has to be a public face to the team and usually this will be the minister. Remember that, whatever the team may like to happen, many people within the congregation, and still more in the wider community, will still regard the minister as the leader and spokesperson for the church.

(c) The minister fails to give any real power to the team members. This inevitably leads to frustration and even anger as team members, who have given up much time to participate, realise that they are being asked to do no more than support the decisions made by the minister or the stipendiary staff. This is an indication of a self-doubting or insensitive leader, and probably indicates that a team should not have been formed in the first place.

The size of the team has an important bearing on its dynamic.

Although management studies about the 'span of control' may not be directly applicable to a leadership team in a voluntary body with mainly part-time members, the findings are instructive. The more complex the task to be accomplished the fewer should be the number of people for whom each leader is responsible. For example the leader of a research team can oversee fewer people than the foreman of a production line. Most studies of the higher echelons of management suggest that a manager should have no more than five or six people directly responsible to him. Experience within the church suggests that a total of six or seven is right. One church with only four said, 'We lack balance and breadth', while another with a team which had grown to 16 said, 'It turned into a committee and we had to scrap it'.[9]

The lines of responsibility must be clearly drawn. If the team is only advisory, then it must be clearly understood by all that decisions are not binding upon the minister, and the discussions may be disregarded when policy is made. However, if the team has real power, then its limits need to be set out with some care:

(a) What happens if the minister disagrees with a decision?
(b) Are team members expected to accept a degree of 'cabinet responsibility'? If so then they are bound by the decisions of the team and should be seen to support them, even though they may have private reservations.
(c) Are individual team members allowed to take independent decisions without reference to the team? In particular, has the minister an authority which enables him to make decisions apart from the team?
(d) Has each team member a particular area of oversight? If so, can the minister also make decisions within that area?

One matter that can cause difficulties in larger churches is the relationship between the staff (who are usually full-time and stipendiary) and the other members of the team. The staff inevitably deal with much of the detail of the everyday running of the church because their whole working time is spent on its affairs. Many policy matters are decided, not by careful cogitation, but by on the spot reactions to particular situations. Other team members need to realise that there is nothing underhand about this. (After all the common law is built up of legal decisions about particular problems.) But the staff have to be very careful to ensure that all matters of real policy are brought to the team meeting to be decided upon. If time was too short and a decision had to be made, then it should be reported to the team.

(4) *Have team members the time to give to being part of the team?* If the majority of team members are not working full-time in the church the amount of time which can realistically be asked of them is very important. If the matter is not addressed members will either find themselves having a breakdown or will withdraw and become part of the team in name only.

How often team meetings are held has to be considered. A recent survey[10] showed 17% of leadership teams met weekly, 33% met twice a month, and 48% monthly or less often. Most of the teams surveyed met for between two and three hours. This is a considerable commitment, and to it has to be added the work which being a member of the team demands. This is especially true if each member has a particular area of responsibility (indeed the time factor may suggest that this should not be the pattern of working). In certain cases the time taken by a person's 'official' position (churchwarden, steward, etc.) has to be added.

What is possible for a limited period may be impossible if it is seen as a 'life sentence'. A limit to the term of office of a team member is desirable – probably a period of three years, with the possibility of a further three if this is agreed by all. This normal term of six years means that resignation after that period is accepted as inevitable, and means a dignified end to the period of office. It may be objected that the person does not lose their charism of leadership just because they are six years older. This is true, but membership of the team should not be seen as the only way in which this charism can manifest itself. Other positions within the church, or in a wider sphere, may be appropriate. Indeed it is part of the *episkope* of the team to seek the guidance of God for the future of each of their members as they reach this stage. It may well be that a well-used 'sabbatical year' which is used for reading and training could be the right preparation for any such wider work.

(5) *Has the minister the necessary skills to work within a team?* This is a serious question. Most ministers were trained to be sole leaders. Many in their formative years admired and attempted to copy men and women of that kind. It is often true that although ministers are persuaded theologically about the rightness of team ministry, they are psychologically unfitted for it. Independence of thought leads to a habit of acting without reference to others. This means that many ministers have to learn a new language when working with a team.

A number of teams have foundered because the minister knew the new language of 'team-speak' but actually operated differently. He or she unwittingly gave two signals. The first is spoken, the second unspoken but no less real and heard just as loudly:

I need you	BUT	Do not come too close
I share your enthusiasm		I am professionally trained
Let us take counsel together		I have greater experience in leadership
I submit to your judgement		I have to carry responsibility for the decision
I have every confidence in you		I am self-sufficient
You are the church		I may leave soon

In 1983 Mark Birchall visited 155 churches where there was some sort of team leadership. They were of different sizes and different denominations. At the end of his investigations he put at the head of his list of 'critical factors': 'the gifts and personality of the minister; his vision for the church, his own ability to develop and lead a team; in particular his willingness to share and to delegate'.[11]

Team leadership has three parts. The first and second are love and wisdom, the third is delegation. The first two shout from the Bible and Christian experience, being the language of respect for each other's ministries, of listening to what others have to say, of ensuring that all are valued, of bearing the burdens and joys of others. The third needs expansion.

Delegation

This is an art which needs to be learnt. It is easy to quote D. L. Moody – 'I would rather set ten men to work than to do the work of ten men' – but most find it difficult to put into practice. Many churches share the experience of one church where growth ground to a halt because the incumbent was unable to delegate, and so kept himself in a lather of busyness doing petty jobs which could easily have been done by others. His churchwarden said in despair, 'He just will not hand over to others.' When a leader says 'I can do it better myself' he is criticising his own failure in selecting and developing the gifts of others.

Many leaders find they come against a deep emotional resistance within themselves in delegating something they started and established. Group Captain Leonard Cheshire spoke of the pain of handing over the running of the Cheshire homes for the terminally ill which he had founded:

We find it both difficult and painful to delegate day to day control of some activity for which we are responsible and which is of importance to us. If it is an undertaking that we ourselves have brought into being, whether in the field of business, social service, or whatever, it may prove almost impossible to force ourselves to hand over the reins because we tend to look upon our creation rather as we would upon our own child . . . We feel that a special relationship has been created, almost a mutual dependency, which we have no right to

disturb . . . such was my experience . . . the act of delegating proved to be a liberating experience.

Many ministers need to enjoy that freedom as their pet projects
are handed over to others, and the potential risks are faced.

Delegation should be seen as an indispensable tool, not
merely to help the leader, but to help the one to whom new
openings and opportunities are being given. 'The development
of your staff is one of your main responsibilities as a manager
and delegation is one way of making sure it happens in a
controlled and useful way.'[12]

Delegation can too easily be done sloppily, so that those to
whom new work is given are unsure of their boundaries, uncertain of the amount of authority they have, and unclear about
exactly what is expected of them. The interview at which
delegation takes place is crucial. There should be plenty of time
for prayer, questions, clarification and, above all, for dreaming
together so that the person catches a vision of the opportunities
of the new work. There are several elements to be considered:

(1) *What is being delegated?* It is impossible to delegate a job
satisfactorily if the scope and nature of the work involved is
unclear to the leader. Before asking anyone to undertake a
particular area of work certain facts about it must be clarified:

What commitment of time does the job require?
What resources are available?
Who is also engaged in the same sphere of work?
How much authority is being allowed – can money be spent,
    people approached to help, publicity distributed, without
    reference to anybody else?
Where can the person seek help if difficulties arise?
Is any training available to help the work to be done better?
What opportunities will there be for review of the work?
    With whom? When?
Is there any term to the work?
Is there anything the person concerned is already doing which
    needs to be dropped to make way for this new enterprise?

Above all the *vision* for the job should be spelt out:

> We are asking you to be a Sunday school teacher so that the young people are taught the faith and find Christ for themselves. We are seeking to increase numbers by 50% in the next couple of years, and the PCC are prepared to give as much help as possible to enable this to happen.

> This is a real opportunity to make a link with a group of unchurched youngsters. They have all sorts of social and spiritual needs. We have not done anything about them so far. Would you like to see what you can do, and we will back you all the way?

> The house group pattern is the main fellowship network of our church and we are asking you to be a leader to enable this group to have a deeper love for each other in Christ, to learn about him, and above all to look outwards to the world more than they are doing at the present.

If the person approached feels he or she is merely being asked to plug a gap because someone has resigned, the work will lack sparkle and they will be unsure how far they can throw themselves into it, and how far they are being backed by the leadership. Further, if they feel that the leader is unsure about what the work entails, and what priority it ought to be given, they will inevitably doubt the amount of support they can expect.

(2) *Who is the right person to whom to delegate the work?* Robert Half gives some cheerless advice: 'There is something that is much more scarce, something rarer than ability. It is the ability to recognise ability.' But it is something which every leader is asked to do.

Some churches have many in the congregation who in their secular lives hold positions of responsibility and influence. But this does not make selecting leaders in the church straightforward. Often such middle-class congregations find that their members have a much lower commitment to the life of the church than less affluent areas.[13] People in such churches live by their diaries, and these are full of appointments for social and pleasurable activities as well as their work. They have much goodwill but are not prepared to drop other engagements to make way for the work of the church. As a result many such congregations find that there is only a small band of overcommitted people who carry the church forward and provide leadership. Further those with clear leadership talents are not always those who have a charism from God. They can run the church like their business, and expect others to carry out their orders, but may not be prepared to accept the hallmarks of Christian leadership – vulnerability and integrity.

One solution, more often adopted in the USA than in Europe, is to 'hire' leadership. Hence a medium-sized church may have a staff of ten or more, each with their particular sphere of activity – youth, single people, assistant pastor, etc. This leads to a church which does not ask for much in terms of personal loyalty and involvement but makes insistent demands for money to maintain the staff. With such a high budget the importance of the 'big givers' is obvious, and too often they can, unwittingly or knowingly, blackmail the church into bowing to their opinions. It enables people to escape the challenge of Christian commitment rather than accept it. In such middle-class churches there needs to be much teaching about the need to be committed to the church of Christ as well as to Christ himself, and the need for people to be unburdened of the 'clutter' which they often gather around their lives. To take the parable of the sower, they are like a cornfield choked with weeds, where 'things' and 'activism' have edged out the living God.

Other churches have few, if any, outstanding leaders. In inner-city and housing estate areas, and in the 'long-grass' rural villages (though not in those which have been swamped by the retired and the commuters), there are few who appear to have natural leadership gifts. But as the Archbishop's Report on Urban Priority Areas (ACUPA) said, 'Not only must local leadership and decision-making be shifted towards those who live in the area, but it must be shifted more to those who belong to the predominant social group.'[14] The report goes on to recommend a Church Leadership Development Programme, which will give people in such areas some basic skills, and, above all, some self-reliance, which will enable them to take positions of leadership. This may well be valuable, but there have been many examples of outstanding leadership being given by people with little natural ability and education, from the apostles onwards. This has come through the recognition of a charism from God, followed by much support and encouragement, usually given *while they are doing the job*. Preliminary training courses before starting are not usually the best way forward for those with little formal education. 'Apprenticeship training' or 'learning on the job' is more appropriate.

Whatever the type of church and the community in which it is set, the choice of people to undertake work is one of the most important decisions facing any leader. The difficulty is that you are trying to see, not only what someone can do, but what they *might be able to do*. You will not be able to judge the rightness of your choice until the person has been some time in the post. This means making a judgement about the future. Inevitably in all walks of life poor choices are often made, as Tacitus said acidly of Galba, 'nobody doubted his capacity to rule until he became Emperor'.[15]

(3) *What support is given to people once they have started a job*? It can too often happen that people undertake something out of goodwill, but with only a hazy idea of what they are about, with no objectives to attain, and with no support on the way. It is like asking someone to climb a mountain without a map, food for the journey or advice.

The sort of support most people do *not* want is constant interference. They need to know that there is someone to turn to if they need help, but otherwise they want to be left alone to get on with the job. As Theodore Roosevelt said, 'The best executive is one who has sense enough to pick a good man to do what he wants him to do and restraint enough to keep from meddling with him while he does it.'

Interference by the leader generally comes about because he is conscious that ultimately he is held responsible for the work. This is right: a leader cannot delegate accountability. He will share the consequences of the other's actions. It is this that can lead to fussy intervention 'so that I shall know what is going on if people ask me'. But it is also a vote of no confidence in the person concerned. There needs to be some way in which, without intrusion, the work can be monitored by the leader.

A regular review of work has been found to be invaluable. The length of time between each review varies according to the person concerned and the type of work. Generally it is found that this 'time span of discretion', i.e. the maximum time there ought to be between reviews, may be several years for senior managers but only a matter of weeks for those who are unsure of themselves and beginning new work.[16]

The leader should be specific about what he wishes to gain from the review. Questions which can be asked are:

What do you feel you have achieved? Has it been what you hoped?

What do you want to achieve?

Do you need any training, either locally or outside the church?

Are there any other resources which you need to do your work?

Are you conscious of growing spiritually through the work?

How long do you want to go on? If you want to relinquish it what would you feel it right to go on to next?

It is sometimes suggested in management circles that the person being reviewed writes a letter setting out his or her answers to the questions above, which is then used as the agenda for the meeting.[17] Although this is certainly not something to impose on everyone, it may well have value in the more responsible positions, not least because some people express themselves more fluently on paper than face to face.

Finally it has to be said that those who need regular reviews more than any others in the church are the leaders, and most of all the minister. He may well want to go to a fellow-minister or to someone in authority in the denominational structure. It is good to see that this is becoming an increasingly common practice in Britain.

Conclusion

(1) This chapter indicates that any attempt to introduce a team leadership (such as 'elders') is a matter of great delicacy and considerable difficulty. A survey of 169 'teams' showed that only three had continued largely unchanged when the ordained minister left and was replaced. What factors make this change apparently so difficult?

(2) The delegation interview is a common experience for all leaders. It is a useful exercise to set out on paper beforehand the matters to be discussed and the aim of the meeting. If there is such a situation in your church likely to arise shortly use that as an example. Otherwise plan an interview with a potential Sunday school teacher or house group leader.

4

The Skeleton

The subject of church structure and government is endlessly fascinating, not least because it is incapable of resolution. The Christian church provides examples of every kind of structure from free-flowing intra-personal groupings to traditional patterns with many centuries of history. It can show structures ranging from those akin to a multi-national corporation to those nearer to a political lobby.

Yet often Christians stoutly deny that their structure is like any 'worldly' model. Therefore they claim that they have nothing to learn from management or 'secular' experience: all they have to do is to follow New Testament precedent. However, what to one Christian is clearly written in the New Testament is less than obvious to another who perceives in its pages a very different paradigm. Even if there was a clear biblical pattern the argument would not be over. Was that pattern merely culturally conditioned, as church government has been down subsequent ages? With hindsight it is easy to see that episcopacy in the Middle Ages reflected the position of the feudal lord, and the congregational principle emerged as democratic views were becoming predominant. Therefore were, say, elders in the New Testament merely a copy of current practice and not for universal adoption?

Some Christians even deny that they have any need for structure at all, calling it 'worldly'. But to say 'we meet as the Spirit leads' denotes the definition of a pattern of working – what management books describe as 'free-flowing'. Structure is as inevitable as the human skeleton and needs to be right – the brontosaurus is said to have been 80 feet long, have weighed

40 tons and have had a brain weighing 3 ounces. His lack of 'government' meant he did not remain relevant to his environment.

The Bible is full of diverse structure. When Moses sensibly listened to his father-in-law and 'chose capable men . . . and made them leaders of the people, officials over thousands, hundreds, fifties and tens', he was setting up a hierarchy.[1] When Paul and Barnabas appointed elders in the newly formed churches of Asia Minor they were following the traditional pattern of the synagogue. Interestingly, for such matters are often not perceived, there is a long discussion in 1 Samuel 8 of a deliberate change of government style – from rule by judges to monarchy.

Most modern writing about the structures of churches is heavily indebted to the work of the Australian theologian Peter Rudge. In his *Ministry and Management* (1968) he identified five possible types of church structures and identified them with particular theological stances.

Eddie Gibbs in *Followed or Pushed* (1987) followed the pattern of Rudge (though giving racier titles to the different models) and added a sixth, 'The Supercharged Community' by which he had in mind the 'charismatic church' which specialises in 'signs and wonders' and a diet of ever more miraculous events. But that description is itself an example of the danger of the systematisation described by Rudge. There never was a church which *only* dealt in miracle. Although these patterns are illuminating, there is also more than a little caricature. No church was ever run purely as a business organisation or was only concerned with human relations. There are churches which tend in one direction or another, but none which only shows one pattern to the exclusion of all others.[2]

In so far as these models show the extremes of possibility, they are useful. But if they are used to label such a complex organism as a local church, and especially if they are seen as prescriptions for future action, they have their dangers. For example, to say that a church is 'traditional' does not mean that only one leadership style will be acceptable, only one way of working will be effective or that all of the congregation think in the same way. It does not describe reality, although it may be a useful shorthand to show the predominant tendencies in the church. These descriptions are instructive in showing the parameters within which churches operate, but should not be taken too seriously.

Doubts about a rigid application of these categories grow when it is remembered that there are many other possible descriptions of organisations. Charles Handy, entertainingly, has four 'management cultures' named after the gods of Olympus.[3] Less colourful was Simon in *The New Science of Management Decision* who introduced an unsympathetic character called 'administrative man', while Van Vleck in 1937 distinguished *Gemeinschaft* from *Gesellschaft*.[4]

But while all are interesting there is a sense of unreality about them for they correspond to no actual organisation. This has been increasingly recognised in various forms of what is called the 'contingency theory' – what Professor Child would describe as an organisation where there is 'a context of multiple contingencies'. Peter Drucker enlarges on this to say 'that there are a large number of variables, or situational factors, which influence organisational design and performance'.[5]

In other words, the structure needs to change in order to cope with developments both within the organisation and in the outside environment. Since the pace of change has increased, is increasing, and looks likely to accelerate further, structures must be adapted ever more frequently to their current surroundings and be ever more flexible. A church which is locked into a certain pattern through organisational arthritis or ecclesiastical fundamentalism will be left behind on the beach as the tide goes out. It can no more survive than a twentieth-century factory which treats its workpeople like serfs or makes widgets which nobody wants.

There is one particular excuse for inertia to which Christian organisations are more prone than most. It is the attitude which says 'it is not the structure but the people who work it which matter'. The underlying presupposition is that we are all nice people and therefore we will get on all right whatever structure we have. But this does not take into account the enormous amount of time and money which can be poured into an inefficient organisation just to keep it going. It is salutary to quantify the cost of a meeting – one diocesan committee recently undertook this exercise and found that to get 15 people together for 2½ hours cost £105 in travelling costs, £28 in secretarial expenses and took 53 hours of Christian time. For a missionary society to have a committee meeting in London for 25 people from different parts of the country may cost over £1000 and take more than 300 Christian hours. Much of this is swallowed up in a semi-voluntary organisation like the church by 'involuntary giving', where people do not realise that they are making a donation to the work of the church simply by attending, but the real cost must be realised.

Nor is it possible simply to let organisation evolve. The only things which evolve spontaneously are disorder, friction and poor performance. Organisations are like cars; they need occasional overhauls. On the other hand they should not always be in the garage being tinkered with. The exception to this rule is the very small church: 'in a very small organisation there will be few, if any, problems of structure. The distribution of tasks, the definition of authority and responsibility, and the relationships between members of the organisation can be established on a personal and informal basis . . . but with increasing size there is a greater need for a carefully designed and purposeful form of organisation.'[6]

But it has to be acknowledged that changing the skeleton of a church can be unnecessary surgery, though intellectually stimulating and itself an exercise in effecting change. One church I visited had spent much of the previous year thinking deeply about the right leadership pattern for them. In fact the congregation was so small that it was a case of 'evangelise or die', and the whole operation had diverted their energies. Indeed I had a suspicion that immersing themselves in thinking about their new structure had been an unconscious evasion of the threatening subject of mission.

Reorganisation can be the last flutter of a dying organisation. Petronius perceived this in AD 66: 'We trained hard . . . but every time we were beginning to form up into teams we would be reorganised. I was to learn later in life that we tend to meet any new situation by reorganising . . . and a wonderful method it can be for creating the illusion of progress while producing inefficiency and demoralisation.' While perhaps too cynical it speaks to the church which prefers to tinker with the engine without putting more petrol in the car, to reorganise rather than getting to grips with the fundamental tasks of prayer and action.

However, while it has to be recognised that rejigging structures does not bring in the kingdom of God or call a single person to Christ, it can lay the foundation from which such mission can spring. If the apostles had not reorganised by appointing deacons to take over part of their work, they would never have been free to give their attention 'to prayer and the ministry of the word'.

A church must not become bemused by structure, so that it is always seeking a perfect skeleton. The best structure does not guarantee results, though a poor structure will always suck into itself too much of the energies of the people with resulting friction and frustration.

There is one fundamental distinction which runs through all the descriptions of different kinds of organisation and which is central to the organisation of the church. It is the difference between the *closed* and the *open* systems.

The closed system emphasises stability and tradition, usually with a strict hierarchy of decision-making and set procedures. There are fixed job descriptions and formal accountability. Above all, only at certain definite points does it interrelate with the outside world. If a business has a closed system the sales force will be the only group to interact with the world outside and within the organisation it will have low status.

The open system is sometimes called 'organic', for the language in which it is described comes from the natural sciences. One of its founders, Ludwig von Bertalanffy, was a biologist. It sees an organisation as always interacting with its environment, in the same way as an animal adapts its actions in response to outside stimuli; it will stress the need for experiment and flexibility, for consultation and team interdependence. There will be considerable personal responsibility placed upon individuals to make decisions and carry them out. Change is seen as 'good' and planning as continuous.

There are few 'pure' examples of either open or closed organisations, but they tend to one side or the other. The closed system is safe and takes no risks, while the open is in continual ferment.

Such theological concepts as the kingdom of God and the Pilgrim People are essentially dynamic and fit more easily into the open system. Indeed Moses was continually reminding the Israelites of the dangers of settling into a closed system once they had occupied the Promised Land. Christians need the stimulus of the outside world or they become either precious or careless. The mission of the church is seen most easily in a church which reflects primarily the open system. However the enticing security of the closed pattern means that we have to struggle to keep the church open to the world; there is a tendency to turn the flower pot upside down again.

Churches need to hear alarm bells when they talk too easily of being in 'a period of consolidation'. Such an expression is often used after a period of mission, when there is a natural tendency to sit back and return to more conventional matters. Unfortunately this necessary breathing space can become a prolonged holiday. The church moves from the open to the closed system. Members become fascinated by its internal workings and over-concerned about their own spiritual temperature; in the Blake-Mouton diagram (Fig. 1) they retreat to a 1,9 position where they create a hospital or superficial, happy family.

It is helpful to examine your own church to see how far it tends towards being either a closed or an open organisation.

Characteristics of Closed and Open Systems within the Church

	CLOSED	OPEN
Mission	Distrust of the 'outside' Allergic to evangelism Little social concern	Interested in the community Bridge builders
Worship	Traditional Emphasis on transcendence of God	New forms not resisted Emphasis on 'God with us' Often joyful
Structure	Go by the book Set procedures Conscious of status Many committees, but . . . Decisions made at the top	Often bypasses legalities Egalitarian Non-hierarchical Uses working parties Decisions emerge from consensus
Innovation	Regarded with suspicion Change is dangerous	Examined carefully Adopted without emotional trauma
People	Congregation seen as support for the clergy Teaching by sermons, planned programmes	Clergy seen as support for the people Teaching by use of experience

The efficiency of a structure can be evaluated. A poor organisation will have:

(1) Friction between different parts of the organisation. This is usually seen when decisions made by one body are contradicted by another. Rival power structures are extremely difficult to handle. Sometimes a business organisation will deliberately establish or inherit more than one decision-making body. This may enable it to generate different sets of options, but it

requires a very strong decision-maker at the top. The difficulties this can cause can be seen in management/union relationships within a business, though the differing viewpoints can be constructive. The church's emphasis on unity makes two parallel power centres almost impossible. Therefore to set up two groups to look at one problem and then choose the best solution is certain disaster in most churches. However it is noteworthy that a 'traditional' organisation can cope more easily than most with different power groupings, because it is more tolerant of blurred boundaries. The Church of England has in the past been an exemplar of this: 'it easily accepts anomaly, and has a rich multiplicity of extraneous organis-ations'.[7] On the other hand it has the disadvantage of such a structure – poor adaptation to change.

(2) Key people thinking about the wrong things. Church leaders should be primarily caring for the flock, both corporate and individual. Business experience would suggest that if they are spending more than a sixth of their time in administrative meetings it is symptomatic of poor organisation.

(3) Too many meetings. Work expands to fill the time avail-able. To have 20 Christian people spend an hour discussing some minor item on an agenda because there is nothing more to do and the meeting must take place is criminal. People become frustrated, and as a direct result these minor points become 'matters of principle' which can be argued about for ever.

(4) Too large meetings. See below for the mechanics of committees.

(5) Lack of a common aim means that the agenda is set by the loudest voice. The usual result is the '20% syndrome': 'we will try to do everything the same only better', which leads to an exhausted church. Mere busyness is no criterion for deciding the effectiveness of a church in the service of God.[8] As Abraham Lincoln said: 'We must ask where we are and whither we are tending.'

(6) Does not alter as growth takes place. A church of 2000 people requires a very different structure to one of 200 or 20. Inappropriate structure can inhibit growth. This is particularly obvious in churches which have a strong congregational principle and seek to involve everyone in all decisions. A group of Baptist ministers felt this was a real constraint on growth. When their 'Church Meeting' became more than 100 strong much time was wasted in deciding simple issues, or in listening to the same malcontents repeating their grumbles.

(7) Lack of creativity. Some structures are black holes from where no new idea ever returns. This is particularly true of bureaucracies: as Derek Sheane of ICI said, 'they can polish but do not invent'.[9] This can be true of churches. Any fresh thinking is met with a padded wall of bureaucratic politeness: 'But we have never done it that way before', 'It might be risky to experiment with something which is untried', 'We shall need to pray very hard about *that* one'.

The committee

The committee as a human structure has had many detractors and some protagonists. It is easy to poke fun at it – 'it takes minutes and wastes hours'. Victoria Pasternak wrote:

> You'll find in no park or city
> A monument to a committee.

But the ubiquity, persistence and sheer numbers of committees should give us pause before declaring them all redundant. They clearly fulfil some need.

A committee is set up in order to hold in balance two factors: the need for people to be represented and the need to make decisions. If the congregational method – where *everyone* is represented – is rejected then some half-way house has to be established if people are to feel at least partly involved with the decisions which are made. Usually some method of election is used to appoint the committee.

But elections have their dangers. Do those elected only see themselves as mouthpieces of the people who elected them? A committee where everyone is merely a representative of a sectional interest has very poor meetings. One church committee I attended worked along these lines. What I was proposing would have caused some little inconvenience to the choir and so Mr X adamantly opposed it: it meant that Mrs Y's house group would have to be postponed for a week and she therefore vehemently contradicted the suggestion 'on a point of principle'. Neither was thinking of the good of the whole church, but only of their own small areas of concern, and what they would say to their constituency.

It is part of the task of leadership to help those who initially joined a committee as representatives to gain a broader perspective. They can then help to broaden the views of those they are speaking for. This can be done partly by people being regular in attending meetings and hearing the discussion of wider topics; but also the agenda needs to have deliberately educational items which enable committee members to learn about and to assess the larger matters which affect the future of the church and community. One PCC I attended sat on hard chairs around a table while deciding business items. After 45 minutes they then moved to a more comfortable room and in a more informal atmosphere had a most perceptive discussion on 'worship'.

Representation has other limitations. Obviously the wider the representation the greater the number of people on a committee. But as numbers grow beyond about 15 the *actual amount of representation drops*.[10] This happens because the committee develops the need for an inner caucus to steer the unwieldy body. It may be called a leadership team, or a standing committee, or just be a group of members getting together before the meeting. It usually develops into the real decision-making body. If so the other committee members will resent losing what they were elected to do – make decisions. The result is that the majority do the only thing they can – sabotage the proposals of the caucus.

The symptom of this process is 'formalisation'. Meetings become increasingly stilted and divorced from the atmosphere of prayer in church on Sunday morning. The degree of formality can be amusing: people who have been calling each other Hilda or Mike five minutes before the meeting start addressing the other as Mrs Jones or Mr Smith once it has begun. But it can be decidedly unamusing, for the formality can be used as a cloak to criticise, run down and destroy others with a vigour (and even vindictiveness) that would never be used outside the meeting. Very often it is women who spot this formalisation, and some of them would say that the committee is an essentially male method of working – with its pretended objectivity and overprecision.[11] Whether or not this is true it is certainly unhelpful to the work of the kingdom.

The non-working of one diocesan committee is illustrative of this process. It had two representatives from each of the 18 deaneries, and (with the ex officio members and secretarial staff) it had a membership of 43. Not surprisingly it was in reality run by a group of five people, all ex officio members. The majority tried to rebel, but there were so many that they achieved no concerted action. Eventually the work of the committee became so predictable that members rebelled in the only way left to them: they ceased to attend. In the end it had to be totally reconstituted because there were not enough members present to form a quorum.

These self-destructive elements pose the question: 'Is the committee a Christian structure?' Is the committee established because there is a lack of *trust* in the people who do the work? Many are elected 'to keep an eye on things'. Certainly the majority of committees polarise into two camps – those who do the work and those who criticise them. Being sniped at by a committee saps the resolve of the most willing person. Such committees are a contradiction in Christian terms. There should be in the church a willingness to see the gifts which people have and then let them exercise them without interference, giving them only that personal support and basic accountability we all need. One church had a Fabric Committee of 13 people.

The secretary convened it every six weeks and duly issued minutes and agendas. The PCC agreed to disband the committee and trust the two people who had done all the work to continue to do it. The result was that the two men rose to the trust that had been placed in their God-given skill and the work was done far better than before with less expenditure of time and nervous energy. One wonders what those master craftsmen Bezalel and Oholiab would have achieved if they had had to be responsible to a committee. Rather Moses recognised that the Spirit of God had filled them and given both personal skill and the ability to teach others. He then affirmed them before the people and let them get on with it (Exod. 35:30ff).

It is also questionable whether the committee is the right pattern for a voluntary organisation like the church. It is always healthier if the people who make a decision have to implement it, if only because they tend to be more realistic. The Christian faith emphasises personal responsibility before God and fellow Christians for our own decisions. For Christians to make decisions which they are not willing to carry out themselves suggests that they are not fulfilling the role of the fellow-servant, but rather showing a master-servant relationship.

If all this can be said against committees why are they still the basic structural building block for virtually all churches? Is it a matter of copying the prevailing pattern of the age, or are they indispensable?

The atmosphere of a decision-making body like a committee is all-important. If members see themselves as a group of friends gathered together to further God's work through prayer, discussion and decision then whether it is called a committee or not is immaterial. But this is not usually how committees are perceived. *A committee works best when it stops acting like a committee.*

Committee members come with differing expectations. Some will expect to work, while others come to sit as passengers, and yet others come to criticise. There should be teaching that no one should join a committee unless they have the time and willingness to be involved with its work. It may be that specialist skills are needed: e.g. in finance, legal matters, buildings. If so then people can be brought in as advisers, but only when their expertise is required. This means that committees should tend to become working parties where each member has a part in the actual work of the group.[12] This in turn will generally mean smaller committees, even if the amount of representation decreases. It is more important that the work is done effectively and efficiently by people who have a good relationship and in an ambience of prayer rather than that everyone should be represented, which is anyway an impossible ideal.

For most leaders the right use of committee structures is an important part of ministry, therefore:

(1) Question the necessity for every committee.[13] How effective is it? Has it the right number of members? How many actually attend? What is the level of trust between its members?

(2) Give teaching on the right attitude of people to decision-making within the church.[14] Remember that those of your congregation engaged in business and administration spend many hours each week in committees or similar groupings. They need to learn a specifically Christian attitude to decision-making.[15]

(3) Teach about the need for people to be committed to the work of groups they join, and emphasise the spiritual nature of such work. Part of this teaching will centre on the need for those with a gift for administration to exercise it. Some have a gift for bureaucracy and can swim confidently in a sea of paper.

(4) Never set up a committee if you can set up a working party, and never set up a working party without specifying when it will end. A committee has an air of permanence which makes it very difficult to dissolve. A working party should have a given task and then expect to terminate.

(5) Never set up another tier of management if at all possible. Every study shows that the more levels of administration there

are the less efficient the organization and the more remote the leadership. Distinguish between 'line' and 'support' elements within the organisation: some parts of the structure deal with its main purpose (e.g. a PCC), while others are supportive of this work (e.g. a prayer group, Diocesan Education Committee). This is not a matter of status or importance but of function.[16]

(6) All structures operate within 'a context of multiple contingencies',[17] and no one structure can cope with every new situation. Flexibility in dealing with new contingencies is usually met by setting up a small sub-unit (typically a working party) to examine, discuss and report back to the main body. Normally its work will be more informal and creative than that of the main structure.

(7) A structure will affect the behaviour of people in it. For example, a highly bureaucratic pattern encourages legalism, petty-mindedness and evasion of responsibility; while a large committee encourages formalism and lack of creativity.

(8) There should be a place in the church for the thrusting entrepreneur, who works by himself, sparkles with new ideas, and is often abrasive in manner.[18] They are often called by God to be evangelists. They need much support and care, but are totally stifled by committee patterns of working.

(9) Do not lightly undertake a change of structure. As Bishop Oliver Tomkins of Bristol said: 'I think the hardest lesson I have learned as a Bishop is the toughness of the materials out of which institutions are made. The amount of spiritual and intellectual energy which has to be generated before one cubic foot of institutional life can be changed seems to be prodigious.' Reorganisation is a form of surgery, and even minor surgery has its risks.

(10) Learn the rules of the game. Some churches have barrack-room lawyers, and most have sticklers for procedure. Leaders should know normal committee procedure and the rules which govern each particular group in the church.[19] Do not formalise

the group by referring to rules yourself, but if a member tries to do this you should know the rule book better than the objector.

(11) Keep the main aim of the group always before it. Vision is as important for a small group as it is for the whole church. And the aim of the group should be related to the overall vision.[20]

(12) It may be helpful to ask a couple of people not to contribute during one meeting but to observe its working and then report at the end of the meeting. Allow time for discussion of their remarks: it makes the members more aware of the ways in which they operate. One Bishop's Council does this and finds it a useful occasional spotlight on its own process of discussion and decision. (Do not overdo this – some groups are overconscious of process and never get down to the business in hand.)

(13) The surroundings in which a group meets, the chairs they sit on, the presence of a table in front of them, the way in which papers are distributed, all affect behaviour.

(14) The role of the chairperson in setting the mood of the meeting is all-important. If he or she is brisk and businesslike, or vague and disorganised, the manner will determine the outcome of the meeting. Some church leaders need to recognise that they are not gifted in this area and should hand over to others, though reserving the right to go through the agenda with the chairperson beforehand. It also has the advantage that leaders can speak more forcefully in support of their own ideas, since they are no longer bound by the need to be impartial.

(15) There are some people who are natural committee people. They are articulate, think on their feet, and choose words carefully. But the slower thinker and the less articulate need to have space given for their views. This is particularly important if there is a wide social mix in the group.

(16) Spot the lateral thinkers. They are the ones who have the

fresh, unusual ideas, come at problems a different way, and often find the way of the Spirit. Many years ago a research scientist at 3M discovered how to make tiny glass beads. Nobody could think of a use for them so he was told to get back to his real work. But as he continued to think inspiration came, and today those little beads are on reflective road signs all over the world.

(17) Committees are better at making decisions than carrying them out. It is here that precision has to be achieved. Seven questions have to be answered:

Who has to know about this decision?
What is the action which is required?
Who is going to carry it out?
By when?
Are there any restrictions (e.g. financial) on those implementing the decision?
Do they have to report back?
How will the committee check that the action has taken place?

Conclusion

It is helpful to sketch out two charts of your church:

(1a) Using straightforward 'boxes' draw up a management chart of the church in the conventional way. All organisations and groups should be included somewhere.
(1b) Using any freeflowing method that suggests itself superimpose on this management chart lines which set out the official *power* and *communication* network. Some method of designating effectiveness should be used: e.g. a dotted line might represent poor communication.

(2) Using a similar method, draw the 'unofficial' power and communication network – if you know it!

Compare the diagrams with the 'Types of Management' table which follows (based on Peter Rudge's work). Which pattern of working is predominant? What are the theological presuppositions of the pattern? How far does the leadership of the church match the expectations of this model? (This may well explain certain puzzling episodes where there has been either friction or an over-ready acceptance of new proposals.)

Title	**TRADITIONAL**	**INTUITIVE**
(Other names)	(Patrimonial) (Gemeinschaft) (System A)	(Charismatic) (System C)
Organisation	Historical Institution Conserving status quo Embedded in society	Spontaneous outburst Centred on leader's perceptions Otherworldly
Leadership Style	Expressing tradition Guardian of truth Age an asset	Prophetic Communicator of enthusiasm Magnetic personality
Minister	Performs the ancient rituals Required to accept norms Eccentricity allowed	High commitment essential Delegation distrusted
Attitude to Change	Pessimistic view of the world Change will be for the worse Conservationist	Change is essential for Intuitive organisation Change expected after lead from minister
Decision-making	Based on custom By 'sense of the meeting' Does not question foundations	Proposed by the minister often without consultation Accept or be excluded

MECHANISTIC	DEMOCRATIC	PROFESSIONAL
(Bureaucratic) (Classical) (System X)	(Human Relations) (System Y)	(Systemic) (Organic) (System Z)
Hierarchical Efficiency-orientated Complex structure	Fluid, imprecise Network of relationships Individualistic	Prepared to change in tune with outside influences
Administrator Directive	Participatory Subject to group goals Articulates feelings	Adapts to change Skilled Highly conscious
Expected to produce results Meticulous attention to detail required	Demand for personal counsel Resolves inter-group tensions	Monitors the organisation Gives wider perspective
Plans are important Thorough investigation of results of change	Seen as threatening group cohesion Accepted only gradually	Continuous adaptation to external pressure Change is necessary
Carefully calculated Detailed directives	Consensus required Decisions emerge from group life	Goals clarified Policy seen in light of goals

Title	**TRADITIONAL**	**INTUITIVE**
Financial Control	Little budgeting Each department has independent accounts New needs met by special appeals Donations haphazard	Projects chosen by leader Appeals for projects Sacrifice demanded
Personnel Management	'Old Boy network' Grooming rather than training	Must share vision of the leader Chosen by leader Sense of vocation to the work expected
Building Policy	Buildings must last for eternity Preservation of the ancient	Aesthetics unimportant Functionality essential Leader is architecturally central
Doctrine of Church	The Israel of God Temple with Priesthood The Holy City	The New Creation New Wine The old superseded
Church and Society	Church enshrines the good in past cultures The Gospel institutionalised	Society under God's judgement Apocalyptic view

MECHANISTIC	DEMOCRATIC	PROFESSIONAL
Centralised Formula to determine contribution	Haphazard 'Give what you feel like'	Giving represents commitment Continuous seeking for new money
Administrative efficiency Appointments made after adverts, short-lists etc.	Amateurish Appointment by election	Commitment to 'partners' required Chosen by interview with future colleagues
Complex buildings for every requirement	Buildings must reflect fellowship Homes used Small rooms rather than halls	Flexibility and mobility looked for
No biblical images fit	The Communion of Saints 'Love one another'	The body of Christ Diversity in a basic unity
Culture must obey the Church Coexistence possible	Christ fulfils society Church is a sign of the Kingdom	Christ transforms culture Church must adapt to the world to do its work

Title	**TRADITIONAL**	**INTUITIVE**
Doctrine of Ministry	Maintenance of ritual and sacrament Educating the young in the tradition	Prophetic call for repentance and faith
Doctrine of God	Stress on Fatherhood God of history Transcendent Creator	Stress on Holy Spirit Christ as discontinuous with past God is irruptive, unexpected in his actions
Doctrine of Man	Pelagian Man is mildly virtuous	Either 'in Christ' or damned Sacraments superfluous

MECHANISTIC	DEMOCRATIC	PROFESSIONAL
Organiser of the institution Manager	Pastor and Counsellor Needs knowledge of human behaviour	Monitors Ministers Maintains
Mechanistic view of universe and its Creator Transcendent	The Spirit within The Father is love without judgement The Son is the Ideal	God is a unity
Original sin means man is lazy and requires coercion	Man is perfectible We need to expand into a greater freedom	Man needs to be truly converted to achieve his potential in Christ

5

Where is the Church?

A recent government report about signposting on the roads of Britain noted that the present signs were very useful if you were on the right route, but little use if you did not know where you were. It therefore suggested that signposts should do more than point to the 'Town Centre', they should say which town!

Churches need to have vision, a focus for their activities. But it is no use seeking the future if they do not know where they are at present.

In 1981 the Church of England asked a group of Christians from overseas to come and assess the national scene. In their report the 'Partners' said that there should be a 'Mission Audit' in every parish in the land. The phrase mission audit then passed into common usage with the aid of a booklet from the Board of Mission and Unity.[1] The intention was to help local churches to see where they were in relation to their community, to evolve a vision for the future, and to see how this could be attained. The word audit was used, despite its financial overtones, because it described well the process which was being called for. It involves on the one hand a deliberate effort to take stock of the present and to try to see where the organisation is going. Further the word audit stems from the idea of 'listening', and an audit is primarily hearing what people and circumstances and God are saying. The church development circle is useful in describing this process. There is no mystique in this; it is automatic in everyday life. For example we *look* in our cupboard and *discover* we have no coffee: we then *arrange* to go to the shop to get some – and then we *do* it (see Fig. 6).

A second strand of thinking has come from the Church

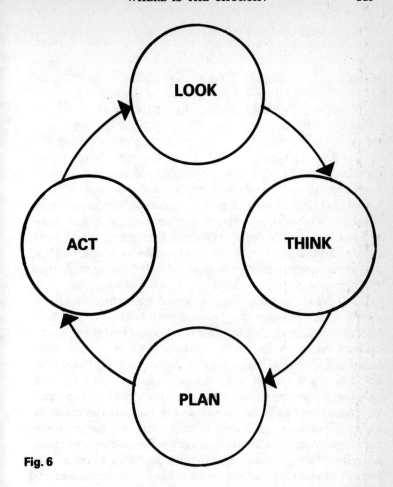

Fig. 6

Growth school. This is associated with the School for World Mission at Fuller Seminary in California. For the last 20 years such people as Donald Magavran, Peter Wagner and, more recently, Eddie Gibbs, have been seeking to identify those ingredients which make a church grow, and those which can hold it back. One of its foundational ideas is that churches ought to *expect* to grow – numerically as well as in other ways. It has been greatly influenced by the Management by Objectives (MBO) methods from management studies, with its emphasis on setting goals and then seeking ways of evaluating progress towards them. In Britain it has been publicised widely through the Bible Society and the Church Growth Association.

Although both means of assessing the work of the church have been criticised, they are certainly right in emphasising the need to discover where the church is and then using that information as a springboard for the future. They have enabled churches to look at themselves critically, with an eye to growth. They prevent pious hope clouding hard fact. A church can too easily live in fantasy. The cruel quip about a minister – 'his church was always growing, but when he left it had fewer people than when he went' – illustrates the dream-world which some can inhabit. It is by no means confined to ministers. In one church I was serving I was so tired of hearing about how the church was packed to the doors in the good old days that I dusted off the old registers and found that in fact the normal congregation was now larger than ever before. It had been packed out – on Mothering Sunday when tickets for the annual outing to the seaside were handed out. The Holy Spirit deals in truth and reality. He brings us down to earth, showing us the truth about ourselves, our churches and the world around us.[2] The Kingdom of God is not built from castles in the air.

Alternatively a church without long-term vision will waste its energies in trying to do a bit of everything and succeeding in very little. Without some overall pattern these actions will often be misdirected expedients and guesses. The church will be run on a series of 'efforts' which leave members tired and disheartened. A church cannot be run by a series of sporadic twitches. Many in management would say that it is better to have the wrong priority than to have none, and the Holy Spirit can take our wrong priorities and turn them to his own purposes, as Saul discovered on the road to Damascus.

Such words as 'assessment', 'accountability', 'audit' sound harsh to some Christian ears.[3] But such judgement has to be a part of leadership – Paul was not backward in trenchantly assessing the spiritual health of the churches in his care. But the most devastating judgements of all occur in Revelation 2 and 3. There, with a divine clarity of vision, the good and bad points of each church are laid bare.

There are dangers in this approach. I find that when I talk to a group of people about this subject there will be some who will grasp hold of the idea enthusiastically, while others will reject it violently. Nearly always this is because they have been exposed to some form of management consultancy exercise at work – and what I have been saying seems to be importing this into the life of the church. Some have had good experiences, while others have found them devastating. In fact Christian assessment is by no means the same as these management exercises. The basis on which they are done is different: management consultants do not have the same set of values, or the same attitudes. In particular they have a different methodology: they are the experts who come in from outside to look at the business, do the investigation, make a report, and collect their fee. In a Christian context the examination of the church is done *by the people in the church*. They may well make use of outside consultants to monitor what they are doing, but the investigative work is done by themselves, and this is in itself one of the most useful parts of any audit.

Above all a mission audit process seeks to find God's pattern for the church. This may or may not involve growth in numbers. But emphatically it should not result in what the vicar wants, or what the power group in the church have been angling for, but in what God wills. If a church embarks on such an assessment without being prepared to go wherever God leads, it had better not start.

Management by objectives

MBO is generally held to have been introduced by Peter Drucker in 1954, and popularised by McGregor and others. It is significant that it came into being at the beginning of a period of great change in industry. During the war objectives had been clear: to make as many tanks, hew as much coal, produce as much steel as possible. Peacetime brought problems. No longer was it enough to go on making more widgets without thought for the future. It was too easy to find that widgets had been made technologically redundant, and along with them all those who manufactured them.

The concept of MBO is simple enough. Any organisation should set itself *goals* which describe the ultimate purpose for which it is set up. These must be distinguished from *objectives* which need to be achieved on the way to those goals. For example, a company's objective may be to make as many widgets as cheaply as possible. But that is not in itself a goal, only an objective which may or may not be correct. If the goal of the company is defined in some such terms as 'to make a profit', then it will need to change its objective if widgets become obsolete, for it will cease to trade profitably. If it confuses the objective with a goal, then it will become obsolete along with the widgets – as firms have found in the textile and heavy industries, where many have been producing goods which no one needed any more.

In attaining the objectives there need to be *policies* – the ways in which the objectives are to be attained. 'Goals' answer the 'why' questions; 'Objectives' answer the 'what' questions; 'Policies' answer the 'how', 'where', 'when' questions.

Drucker also said that goals had to be both quantifiable and attainable. Otherwise they became vague generalisations which can never be checked. To set a goal of 'making a profit' is easily judged by looking at the bottom line of the balance sheet.

How far is MBO applicable to the church? In its early days the Church Growth school tended to accept it uncritically, and churches were asked to set down their goals in easily quantifiable terms: to 'grow by 15% a year', 'to bring 10 new people to Christ each month'. Often there was a tendency to blur the distinction between goals and objectives, and at times an over reliance on what could be counted.[4] At the same time it has done a great service to the church in making it look carefully at its life, and not to see facts and figures as 'unspiritual'. What Paul said about his own life is true of the church: 'I do not run like a man running aimlessly: I do not fight like a man beating the air'.[5] Just as industry needed MBO to assess what it was doing and think ahead when it entered a period of change, so the church needs some form of self-assessment for the same reason. But the criticisms which have been made of MBO recently in management theory have modified it extensively. Indeed it has lost much of its fashionable appeal as a prevailing philosophy.

The most important criticism is the realisation that organisations do not have goals, only people do. While it is possible to write down a goal for an organisation it is human beings who work within it. And individuals may well have different drives to the goals of the organisation.[6] These can work in opposite directions and produce much conflict. If a company sets itself the goal 'to make a profit' while its employees see their goal as 'to get as much money as possible for our work' there is a potential battleground. The same can happen within a church. Often there is an unwillingness to admit to private drives. A congregation may happily agree that the church's aim is to worship God, but if they really want it to be the best social club in town there is likely to be trouble. This discrepancy between public pronouncement and private (even unconscious) expectation is common. A group of people will readily say 'we need to read the Bible more', but then absent themselves from the church Bible study because they have other drives which are dominant – laziness, personal animosity to some there, pursuit of a hobby. It was not hypocrisy to affirm a wish to read the Bible, but there were stronger pressures in their lives.

It is not only in the congregation that there may be a divergence between the stated goals of the church and the personal aims of individuals. The leadership themselves may have their own difficulties with the agenda of the church. They may be afraid of the dissension which seems likely; they may be looking for their next job; they may be experiencing some crisis of faith. There is a host of possible reasons why their personal drives may differ from the stated aim of the church although they had a hand in framing it, and continue to declare it to the people. And this also is not hypocritical: personal aims do not necessarily have to coincide with those of the church. While leaders should be aware of their own drives and ambitions, they should also be prepared to continue to proclaim clearly the goals which God has given for the church.

A second criticism which has been made is that it is not always possible to set a goal which is both measurable and attainable in a certain time. A company may have as a goal 'to become a world leader in the research and development of new drugs'. Assessing such a goal will clearly bring in many subjective elements, the medical value of the drugs produced, the strength of the competition etc. which make mathematical exactitude impossible.

It is likely that in the church a quantifiable and attainable goal will be unusual. Indeed it may be that therefore the word 'goal' should be dropped, for it suggests things which can be measured and work which can be completed. Such words as 'vision' or 'focus' or 'direction' are more satisfactory, and more accurate in describing the answers to the 'why?' questions.

One church set out its vision as being 'to reflect the life of the Gospel', but that is hardly either measurable or capable of being finally attained. But this did not make it useless. Indeed it was consideration of that vision which led to many objectives being set: to become more aware of the community, to become closer to God, to evangelise, etc. These objectives led in turn to policy decisions: to find out where people met in the vicinity of the church, to set up a course on prayer, to establish nurture groups for enquirers and young Christians. Without the vision there would have been no focus for action, and the church could have descended into purposeless activism.

By its nature vision will change with time, and certainly the objectives which strive towards it will alter. Just as Paul knew that personally he had not yet arrived, but he pressed on 'towards the goal'[7] so we need to have a vision for the church; not that we shall eventually 'arrive' at it but that we may have it constantly before us. It is not a will o' the wisp but a guiding star; we do not read that the Israelites ever touched the pillar of fire and smoke, but they could not have done without it.

The third criticism is that nearly always the quantifiable and supposedly attainable goals favoured by MBO are not achieved in practice. This leads to feelings of failure and a disheartened management. Etzioni says, 'the goal model approach results in attention being focused on the organisation's lack of success in attaining goals at the expense of more meaningful forms of analysis'.[8] The same can be said of many churches which set themselves goals of this kind. Sometimes the goals are unrealistic, sometimes they are overtaken by events. The usual reaction is to bury the experience. It is common for a church, after a conference at which it sets goals, for it never to allude to them or the conference again. Without this essential feedback which should lead to evaluation and the setting of further goals, MBO is dead.

Vision

If Management by Objectives gives us a flawed answer, what is a suitable alternative? I would suggest that there are certain necessary parts in the establishing of a vision for a church or Christian organisation. This must be the overarching will of God for the church and the community in which it is set.

Leaders often wonder when is the best time in their ministry to lead a church to embark on such a voyage of discovery. This can happen at any time but there seem to be two golden periods. The first is when a new minister has been in post for about a year: he is established and needs to help the church to own a common aim so that they can go forward together; he is also still sufficiently new that anything wrong with the church is not yet his fault. The second is when a minister has been in his church for ten years or so, by which time he has used up most of his bright ideas and the church is long over its honeymoon relationship with him. There is a need for new thinking and fresh definition of direction. However an audit should not be limited to these periods. If no similar exercise has been carried out in the last three or four years there is a prima-facie case for having one.

Vision should be God-given, but that must not be an excuse for expecting God to let us off the necessary homework. Romans 12:1,2 gives us a recipe for discerning the 'good, pleasing and perfect will' of God.

First there must be the consecration of the church to seek the will of God: 'Offer your bodies as living sacrifices . . . which is your spiritual worship' – note that this is *corporate*. One church designated a special period in which forgiveness was sought for past over-critical attitudes within the church, reconciliation between those at variance was encouraged, and special prayer was offered both at routine services and at special prayer meetings. Other churches have used less elaborate methods; but the end has to be the same: a genuine preparedness by at least the bulk of the congregation to seek the will of God, and having found it to obey it.

This God-centred start must be made, or all that comes afterwards will degenerate into a piece of management theory or a power struggle. The prayer will seek the clear-sightedness given by the truth-revealing, reality-bringing Holy Spirit.

Secondly there has to be careful consideration of the present situation in ways which are not squashed into the 'pattern of this world', but 'transformed by the renewing of your mind'.[9] The culture in which we exist and the personal objectives that we have should be those of the Kingdom and not of the world around us, otherwise we shall not look at the church with the loving eyes of God but with the calculating eyes of an accountant. The church should seek to get God's mission audit on its affairs. An anonymous executive remarked that 'to look is one thing. To see what you look at is another. To understand what you see is a third. To learn from what you understand is still something else. But to act on what you learn is all that really matters.' The Christian needs the help of the Holy Spirit to lead through all these stages.

Whenever feasible this thinking should be done by as many people within the church as possible. It makes the church more self-aware and more cohesive. No longer does Mrs X only know about the evening service and the Women's Bright Hour that she personally attends; she participates in the audit and learns that the youth group is thriving but the numbers at the morning service are declining, that the divorce rate in the area is one in three and the local schools are poor in their teaching of Christianity. She may even come to a realisation of the complexity of the situation facing the minister, and be more charitable in her assessment of him in the future.

There are many ways in which this self-knowledge can be obtained. Probably the most popular is some form of written audit of the church. The Church Growth literature sets out many patterns; a fuller list is given in the BMU *Mission Audit* booklet, and there are helps given by denominational authorities.[10]

Figure 7 summarises the process of an audit and suggests the questions to be answered. As part of this process it is important to decide whether or not outside consultants are to be used.[11] It is generally found that trained 'outsiders' can monitor and encourage an audit in a way that is not possible if it is done internally. There are certain reasons for this:

(1) Outsiders can comment in ways that would be too difficult for those within the church: they also act as lightning conductors, and any anger which is generated is focused on 'those from outside' rather than being turned destructively inwards.

(2) The outsider's eyes can often pick out things in the church with which those within have become so familiar that they no longer see them, like that mark on the wallpaper at home which you no longer notice. A church, like every human grouping, evolves (unknowingly) certain routines and ways of behaving. Many of these are no more harmful than the personal idiosyncrasies we all evolve in the way we brush our teeth or sit in a chair. But some can be offputting for newcomers or directly

A POSSIBLE PATTERN FOR A
MISSION AUDIT

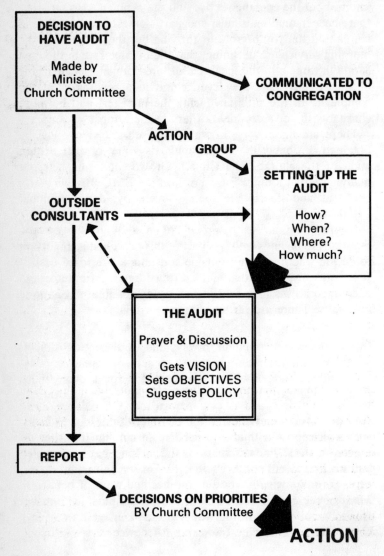

DECISION TO HAVE AUDIT

Made by Minister Church Committee

COMMUNICATED TO CONGREGATION

ACTION GROUP

OUTSIDE CONSULTANTS

SETTING UP THE AUDIT

How?
When?
Where?
How much?

THE AUDIT

Prayer & Discussion

Gets VISION
Sets OBJECTIVES
Suggests POLICY

REPORT

DECISIONS ON PRIORITIES
BY Church Committee

ACTION

Fig. 7

harmful. One church I visited had the custom of locking the door immediately the service began in order to encourage punctuality in the congregation, but it also had the effect of shutting out the timid stranger.

(3) The views of an outsider are often seen as carrying more weight than those within the fellowship. They can affirm all the good things in the church, for too often audit is seen as being merely critical; at its best it encourages and establishes all that is sound and wholesome.[12]

(4) The outsiders become the recipients of much that is hidden under the surface. For this reason the confidentiality of those who do the audit must be known to be absolute. Grievances are not confined to the people articulating them – they are a 'social event' of significance in the life of the church.[13]

(5) The outsiders should have particular skills which enable the audit to be more thorough, and knowledge of resources which can suggest possible ways forward once the vision has been grasped.

Against this it has to be said that such consultants can sometimes inhibit, particularly in UPA parishes where it is easy for them to be seen as yet more 'inspectors' sent in by the authorities. For this reason they must be seen as Christian friends invited by the church to help it to do its work, rather than snoopers trying to find skeletons in the cupboard. It is unrealistic to imagine that they will be totally neutral and objective: that is impossible and is best recognised. On balance most churches would find the use of consultants helpful in most circumstances, and if the possibility of an outside view is rejected a church should make sure that the reasons for that decision are sound and not just a device for protecting themselves from the truth.

It is surprising how often a careful examination of the present situation enables a church to begin to see in outline God's plan for the future. One church looked at its own life and that of its community and realised that only 0.8% of the population in its parish went to *any* church. It required no great flash of inspiration to see that its vision had to be found in the area of mission. This in turn led to the setting of certain mission-related objectives. It was then possible to formulate the policies which tied these objectives down to diaries, places and people.

Questions about the entry of members of the congregation into the Christian faith are always important. A recent survey done among 400 people from various churches in my own area suggested that 75% of members had been brought up in the life of the church; 80% had some sort of 'turning to God'; but 60% of them described this experience as 'gradual' (the likelihood of a gradual conversion increased with age); the most common age for those recently converted was the late 20s or early 30s. In answering the question, 'What was the main factor under God which led to this?' 45% spoke of the influence of a friend or relative; 16% mentioned the personal influence of a minister at an important time in their lives; 15% had been asked to join a group or organisation; 11% saw an evangelistic event as crucial; and 13% cited a multitude of other factors.[14] Such figures give a solid foundation upon which to evolve a strategy for mission in the neighbourhood.

Although facts about congregation growth, other denominations, church organisations, the community, are important, the less obvious facts can be yet more significant in discerning the vision for the church. For example, I often find that asking recently arrived members of the congregation about their reasons for attending are highly important. If they transferred from another church, why did they come to this particular church? If they have entered into faith and therefore attend the church, what means did God use to bring them to faith? What was their particular faith journey? How easily did they find a place in the congregation? One church had had no one added to its number for more than five years – that was very revealing of its poverty of outreach.

In the life of a church feelings may be as important as facts. People's opinions should be sought, especially those who do not figure in the places of power: the young, the very elderly, those on the fringe, often communicate more of the real motivations of the church than those more at the centre of things.

Beneath the surface of every organisation there is power – an audit needs to reveal where this lies. Where are decisions really made? What pressure groups are there? Which individuals are using their church membership to forward their own ego? This is to be expected. There were personal and factional rivalries in the New Testament church. The 'political' view of organisations sees them only in terms of competing power groupings, and excludes tolerance, compromise and the finer human feelings. Nevertheless there is enough truth in it to make the power diagram an important element in an audit.[15]

Questions about prayer and worship are even more important than questions about organisations and leadership structures. Members of congregations involved with an audit are often very willing to confess their shortcomings and needs in such matters. This is particularly true if an unsigned questionnaire guaranteeing confidentiality is used. Often it is found that there is a deep spiritual hunger for a genuine knowledge of God and for reality in prayer which is not being met by the routine of the church's life.

But audit is not just a matter of finding out the facts about the present. That may be interesting but cold. It is also a matter of dreaming dreams, of using imagination, of inspiration and insight. There are various ways in which people can be encouraged in this:

(1) In a group, after spoken prayer, allow a time of silence – possibly prolonged – after which members contribute what they felt God was saying to them about the church and its future. The group must have someone with discernment to distinguish faith from fantasy, and the wholesomeness of truth from personal axe-grinding. Sometimes one of the gifts of the Spirit, especially prophecy, will be used. Here too discernment is necessary, remembering the warning of Bishop David Pytches

that no prophecy is better than 80% proof, and it is always necessary to sift out the human element.[16]

(2) Since present problems and personalities can prevent people from seeing the distant horizon, it can help to ask, 'What would you like this church and community to be like in ten years' time?' For people who find the distant future difficult to imagine this can be a useful widening of possibilities.

(3) Alternatively, constructive dissent can sharpen focus, prevent sloppy thinking, sharpen issues, suggest different courses of action. A leader who surrounds himself with 'yes-men' shows his own insecurity. The stronger leader looks for 'no-men' who will complement rather than be pale reflections of his or her own ministry. If there is no disagreement, wait until there is. Alfred Sloan of General Motors, who successfully challenged the supremacy of Henry Ford, once said after the board had meekly agreed to a course of action, 'I propose we postpone further discussion of this matter until our next meeting, to give ourselves time to develop disagreement and perhaps gain some understanding of what the decision is all about.'

(4) The imagination is almost always visual; we dream pictures not words. Therefore to encourage people to draw, however inexpertly, what they see for the future can be a useful means of unlocking their spirits. When this is a group exercise on a large scale – a wall half covered with newsprint, for example – it can be great fun and lead to much excited discussion. A more formal extension of this is the use of diagrams and graphs which can say more than many words.

(5) Above all, most people think in story. We often visualise a good story to ourselves as it unfolds. Christ used it to communicate and we should treasure the stories of our church, whether it be those tales of the past which are part of the folklore of the place or dreams of what might yet come to pass. In the telling of story the imagination is free. In some ways the stories looked for in an audit are something akin to science

fiction, the tales of what-might-be, the narratives of a never-never land which might just possibly come true. They quicken the imagination and help people to think new and wider thoughts.

But although the imagination is powerful it has always to be remembered that to walk into the future means leaving the present behind. Things which become outworn must be discarded. Voluntary societies find this intensely difficult, whether it be the scout movement abandoning their wide-brimmed hats, or a missionary society realising that its work is complete and a new indigenous church has been formed. Some churches are so loaded with the impedimenta of the past in the form of unnecessary organisations, unwanted buildings and inappropriate posts that they can hardly move. To enter into an audit without being aware of the pain which uncovering the moribund may cause is unwise.

Nowhere is this more obvious or more difficult than when it applies to people: 'individuals may be described as obsolescent when they are so hidebound in vision, adaptability, and application that they cannot cope with the situations and decisions of working life'.[17] But it must be tackled. George Marshall, Chief of Staff in the Second World War, remarked that he had 'a duty to the soldiers, their parents and the country to remove immediately any commander who does not satisfy the highest performance demands . . . It was my mistake to have put this or that man in a command that was not the right command for him. It is therefore my job to think through where he belongs.' Japanese industry seldom fires anyone; they move them side-ways, so that at least they have the status of 'counsellor'. In voluntary organisations no painless way of moving people who are suffering from obsolescence has been found, except the possibility of 'terms of office', by which it is understood that someone will resign after a certain number of years in a post.

It also has to be borne in mind that any vision may be wrong. We have a lust for certainty, but God treats us as adults and will not allow us this ultimate luxury. We pray, we investigate and think, but in the end we may make a mistake. An audit is not a forecast of the future. Our own emotions and enthusiasms are so strong that the perfect will of God may be obscured and we think we are doing his will and we are not.

The pathway of Christ for our church is there. Like the route up some Himalayan peak the vision is glorious but remote, sometimes clear, but often shrouded in the clouds. However, without those glimpses, and the tales of those who have gone before, we shall never even start.

The vision is there, not clearcut maybe, but perceived. The next questions to be answered begin with 'what?' – 'What are we to do to attain the vision?' The objectives have to be spelt out. A maze in a puzzle book is more easily solved if you start where it says 'finish'. Critical Path Analysis suggests the same, and so does common sense.[18]

Sometimes the objectives flow fairly easily from the vision. One church found its vision to be: 'in Christ, to serve the community'. As this was already the direction they were pointing, to set objectives was comparatively easy – they agreed fairly quickly to review their current activities and see if there were any gaps which they should be filling.

At other times there needs to be much further thought. Up some mountains there is only one feasible path, while others have a multiplicity of possible routes. A church which sets its vision as 'to evangelise the parish' may not find it easy to answer the 'how' question. There are so many possible ways of evangelising, so many methods on the market, that it can be bewildering. It is often useful to go back to the investigative work done as part of the audit. Some of the facts uncovered there may show where the objectives lie. If it showed a low level of interest in the local community, few bridges into it, and a self-satisfied congregation, the objectives will be very different than if the audit had shown a congregation filled with the enthusiasm of the Spirit and longing to share what they have learned of God with their neighbours.

Churches which have undertaken an audit tend to set themselves too many objectives. Resources of people and money are limited. A host of good suggestions can swamp reality – one church produced over 200 from their seven discussion groups! There has to be a setting of priorities and a discarding of ideas which may be useful but not immediately relevant. It is easy for the good to become the enemy of the best at this stage.

Churches also need to remember that time is as much a resource as money or anything else. Not everything has to happen immediately, nor should it. Business reckons that 10 years is not unusual for a big project to come on stream, and school advisers do not look for the results of an assessment until five years have passed.

For these reasons the decisions about 'objectives' need to be taken with proper regard to the decisions about 'policy'. However all the time the priority of the objectives has to be seen to be paramount. If an objective is right then it should not be held back by apparent difficulties of implementation. If churches only went ahead when they had all the resources at their disposal few would move at all. Again and again as churches have ventured forward in what they believe is God's path they have found that apparent lack of money or people has been made good. Down the ages the church has found the truth of Christ's words: 'Seek first his kingdom and his righteousness, and all these things will be given to you as well'.[19] There is no such thing as a new initiative without risk, for it commits our present resources to an uncertain future. Without adventure there is only rigidity.

For many leaders it is the risk which looms largest. They are conscious that if a project fails, if people are upset, if things go wrong it is they who will be blamed. They can console themselves with the words of Peter Drucker: 'The better a person is, the more mistakes he will make – for the more new things he will try'; and the saying attributed to Rabbi Israel Salanter, 'a rabbi whose community does not disagree with him is not really a rabbi; and a rabbi who fears his community is not really a man'.

It is encouraging to remember that an Apollo rocket reaches the moon only after a multitude of small corrections of small mistakes – they veered off course but then a command from Houston brought them back on track. The mistakes did not matter. Provided they reached their final goal of moon orbit the errors were insignificant. Some can be so fearful of getting it wrong that they never achieve lift-off.

Conclusion

(1) Has your church had any form of assessment during recent years?

(2) Are there outside consultants who might be helpful in joining with the members of the church in examining its life or some part of it?

(3) Is it possible for the church leaders to spell out the *vision* they have for the church, the *objectives* they need in order to move towards the vision, and the *policies* which are being adopted to reach the objectives? If so: Who else knows about them? Do these people agree with them? Have they been recently reviewed?

(4) It has been said that churches 'expect too much in the short-term and not enough in the long-term'. Does your church allow seeds to grow naturally, or expect them to 'spring up immediately' – and then find that they wither?

6

Changing Things

Wherever the Holy Spirit moves there will be change. We who look for a 'new heaven and a new earth' cannot complain that there may be some alterations to the scenery along the way. The Bible is full of people taking new initiatives under the guidance of God. From Abraham setting off into the unknown to a frightened Ananias making his way to Straight Street there is a glorious medley of folk undergoing and initiating new things.

Change is dangerous. Moses thought so as he approached Pharoah, and Paul thought so as he made his way 'with much trembling' to Corinth (1 Cor. 2:3). Christian leaders down the ages have found that proposing and implementing change is hazardous work. They need the necessary skills, bathed in prayer.

A church is a corporate body. It is therefore essential for a leader to ensure that the vision which he or she is seeking to convey to the congregation becomes effective in practice. Objectives have to be set and policy decisions approved. Every church has some sort of decision-making process – PCC, church committee, trustees, congregational meeting, etc. – and it is in getting agreement and implementing plans that much of a minister's life is spent.[1]

Unless it is decided to 'remain as we are', all decisions involve change.[2] Implementing decisions in a church usually means changing the attitudes and behaviour of people so that they know what is being proposed and become enthusiastic about it. This is a matter of using the proper means of communication: 'tell people and they forget; show them and they remember;

133

involve them and they are committed'.[3] This has to be done with courtesy and sensitivity, because many people find change stressful and need reassurance throughout the period.

There is an uncertainty in change for it opens out new vistas. This unpredictability excites some, while others would echo the resigned comment of Washington Irving: 'There is a certain relief in change, even though it be from bad to worse, as I have found in travelling in a stage coach, that it is often a comfort to shift one's position and be bruised in a new place.'[4]

Very few changes do not have a downside. Unless these negative aspects are taken into account there will almost certainly be strong resistance, and much of it will be justified, for alterations cannot be introduced without taking into account the human nature of those it affects. This is particularly important because *the negative results of a change are usually apparent before the benefits become evident*. I recently visited a church which had grown so much that it needed to extend the building. As I stood in the middle of the rubble and the dust of the half-gutted church, the vicar told me he had to remind people constantly to keep the vision of the new and finer building before their eyes while they endured the inconvenience of the present.

The importance of discontent

It is all too easy for leaders to introduce changes without the people they are seeking to influence being aware that there is any need to change. The leadership will have spent long hours thinking around a problem; books will have been consulted, and visits may have been made to churches where similar problems have been overcome. In the process they may well have almost forgotten *why* they wanted to make the change in the first place, and become captivated by *how* it is going to happen. In fact they are proposing change because they are *discontented* with the present situation.

It is part of our human nature to become enthusiastic about

the suggestions we make. This is a real danger for we can reinforce positive drives for change without considering the negative aspects. If leaders fail to look at the reasons for *not* adopting their ideas, constraints will eventually balance positive drives and nothing will be achieved. It can too often happen that ministers put forward a suggestion with great force, especially if they feel that it is the will of God, without thinking about the process by which they came to that decision themselves.

It is almost too obvious to state, but people will not want change unless they are conscious of a problem that needs solving. *The amount of discontent with the present dictates the amount and pace of change which can be introduced.* Unfortunately many leaders give answers to questions which people have not yet begun to ask.

It is all-important to take people through the same process that the leaders went through: defining the problem to be solved; considering a variety of possible solutions; choosing one particular solution after considering the negative as well as the positive factors involved. Much time has to be spent with those who are to share in the decision (PCC, mission committee or whatever), spelling out the perceived problem. It may be that others do not see that there is a difficulty. This is especially true if there is an implied questioning of the traditions of the past or a suggestion that the work of an individual is less than perfect. The decision-makers have to realise that there is a problem which needs addressing. The Old Testament prophets wanted change – sometimes they looked for inward repentance, and sometimes for political change. It is noticeable that they spend much time explaining what is wrong, before they go on to suggest a solution.

But the recognition of a problem is not in itself enough. There also has to be enough discontent with the present. Many congregations recognise that they ought to have more people worshipping with them on a Sunday morning, but are not sufficiently discontented with the present to have enough drive to make necessary changes. This leads to the common attitude, 'yes, we ought to have more young people in our church but they will have to take us as we are'. There has to be an unfavourable judgement on the present to make it possible to introduce change.

This is a matter of everyday life. As we look at our living-room we may say, 'this carpet is scruffy'. The problem has been recognised. But there may not be sufficient dissatisfaction with the situation to do anything about it. Inertia, insolvency or even nostalgia ('It was given to us as a wedding present') may militate against anything happening.

But it is not true that the more discontent the greater the possibility of change. The Mouton diagram describes a very important process (Fig. 8). The 0,0 position shows that where there is no discontent there is no possibility of change. As the level of discontent increases so the possibility of change increases – up to a certain point. But if the change is not made at the right time the nature of the discontent changes. From an unease about a particular situation it changes into frustration with the leadership and depression settles over the church. The

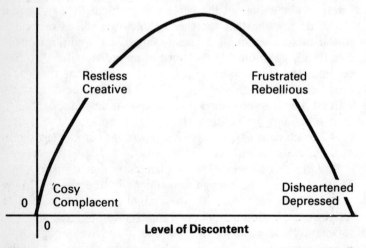

Fig. 8

confidence of the congregation is severely shaken. Some will feel they have successfully scotched an attempt to impose a change they disliked and others will feel the leadership has been weak in not changing the situation when it was possible. Timing is all-important in the management of change. The situation is a dynamic one and can be illustrated by a series of diagrams. In Figure 8a the familiar pear-shape begins to show itself. Some are anxious for change, but there is a considerable 'tail' of those who are unsure or in opposition. Either they do not recognise that there is a problem to be solved, or they disagree with the solution which has been proposed.

The situation has developed (8b). There are now some who are becoming frustrated because the change has not already been made and moving into the 'rebellious' quadrant. However the bulk of the people are now at the point where they are saying 'we have got to do something about it' and will accept change. There are still a number of people at the 0,0 position. It is wrong to wait until they are convinced – they are unlikely to accept change while it is still being discussed. They *may* fall in with it once it has happened and they can see the advantages. *This is the time when change can be most easily introduced.*

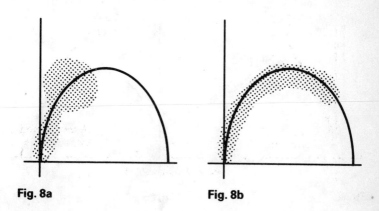

Fig. 8a   **Fig. 8b**

> There is a tide in the affairs of men
> Which, taken at the flood, leads on to fortune;
> Omitted, all the voyage of their life
> Is bound in shallows and in miseries.
> On such a full sea are we now afloat,
> And we must take the current when it serves,
> Or lose our ventures.
>
> *(Julius Caesar)*

It is interesting to see what 'miseries' happen when an opportunity for change is not taken 'at the flood'. The best time for change has been missed (8c) and the majority of people are now feeling discontented since nothing has happened. Those who were against change are becoming confident that they have won a 'victory'.

The final position (8d): the church settles into two camps with little communication between them. At worst a situation of trench warfare begins between the two sides. Because the change was *not* made the congregation has become divided, and the competence of the leadership called into question. *The church has been divided by doing nothing.*

It is clear that during this period the object of the discontent has changed. Initially there was dissatisfaction about some problem in the church. By the time the final stage is reached the prime unhappiness is about the standard of leadership. For this

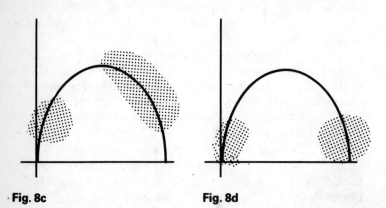

Fig. 8c   **Fig. 8d**

reason members of the congregation will be much less ready to embark on any other venture.

The elements of change

One church may introduce a major change with hardly a ripple, while in another a minor alteration means a crisis. It is important to recognise what the change means to the people concerned, and this cannot be confined merely to the rate of change etc. It also has to take into account the morale of the church and the feelings of the people. The elements of change can be taken as being: Magnitude, Speed, Direction, Threat to status, Confusion, Misunderstanding, Drive.

Magnitude. Too much change overwhelms people. Some churches become bewildered and bruised because too many changes have been introduced too quickly. There may be times when the situation is so perilous that desperate measures have to be introduced. If the position is seen to be as critical as that of the Anglican Church in Canada has been, then its words will be echoed: 'We do not advocate change for the sake of change. We see change as the condition for survival.' When there is a fire there is no time for niceties, but only in such an extreme situation should this happen. Revolutions are notorious for producing consequences which their originators do not expect.

The danger of submerging people in excessive change has to be borne in mind particularly when introducing the vision which is perceived as being right for the church. 'A leader with a clear vision gives his people a true sense of destiny . . . a true taste of God's glory.' But vision can be overpowering.[5] There may be a flight into fantasy leading to euphoria and unreality among some and irrational opposition from others. It is important not only to spell out the overall direction but also the first steps to be taken to attain it. Vision there must be, or proposals seem a bunch of unrelated and unnecessary changes, but it must be introduced gradually and reiterated often. The disciples were notoriously slow at picking up the vision which Christ put in front of them.

Where the morale of the church is low because of decline or a recent trauma, people are reluctant to 'think big'. This is also true of many UPA parishes, where the time horizon is short and people live a hand to mouth existence on their dole money. In these situations, there needs to be a mention of wider goals, but decisions should be restricted to what can be accomplished in a short period *successfully*. In a situation of failure, immediate, highly visible success can have a tonic effect. A financial boost, or decorating the church can open up new possibilities and help the congregation to see that they need not despair of the future. Such churches need small changes in a consistent direction.

Speed. There has to be a balance between the need for change in order to meet new challenges, and at the same time an atmosphere of stability and continuity in the interests of existing members. The congregation will become disorientated if change is introduced too quickly. Jesus' disciples showed every sign of being so emotionally overwhelmed by the changes they had experienced from Palm Sunday to Good Friday that they were unable to comprehend any new idea – let alone one as shattering as the Resurrection.

On the other hand if change is too slow the congregation will not be aware that anything is happening and feel unhappy because 'nothing is being done'.

Direction. It is easiest to do more of the same. If there is a youth club in a church it is not difficult to suggest an enlargement of its present pattern of work. It is more difficult to suggest that its work be substantially changed: e.g. from being a 'closed' to an 'open' club. It is even more difficult to suggest that it be shut and the work among young people take a completely different path. The wider the deviation from the present direction the greater will be the tendency to resist change. As on the road, U-turns should only be attempted with great care.

It is comparatively easy to assess the above factors to determine how large a change is being suggested. Indeed they can be quantified on a 1 to 10 scale with reasonable accuracy. However, it is the non-quantifiable factors which are the most important, and they all stem from fear. A degree of fear and tension is inevitable and cannot be avoided. But it is important for a leader to be aware of what kinds of fear are being aroused by the proposals for change.

Threat to status. Many people find that they are valued in the life of the church in a way which does not occur outside. This can be creative and upbuilding as the Christian fellowship acts to encourage the development of its members. However it can be perverted into a petty office-seeking which becomes hungry for power however insubstantial. If a change is seen as threatening the position of either an individual or an organisation there will be added stress. For example, if a proposed leadership team threatens the position of the church committee or PCC, or a new member of the church stands for election to an office in the church, then a threat to the status quo will be present and negative emotions will surface (or, more likely, remain just under the surface).

Confusion. Change makes people bewildered. They perceive that they are losing the familiar scenery and are being rushed into a place where they do not feel safe. Proverbs 22:28 commands us: 'Remove not the ancient landmark' (AV). Leaders sometimes have to, but it must be done with great care and compassion for those who will be upset. Bewilderment leads to feelings of helplessness which in turn arouse anger, dread, depression, frustration. These will often be directed against a person or group. This is especially true of those with suppressed anxieties in their own lives. A wise leader will ensure that dissent is seen to be welcome, and will not be regarded as disloyal for a 'loyal opposition' can be most constructive. There are very few ideas which are so well formed that they cannot be improved by helpful criticism. Indeed if there is little discussion and a plan is too easily accepted it suggests that it is not properly understood and opposition will arise in the future when the real implications are realised. Confusion can be overcome in part by enabling people to participate in the process of change rather than dumbly acquiescing because they do not understand what is going on.

Misunderstanding. Knowledge gives a sense of control while uncertainty brings fear. Whenever change is being discussed there will be those who do not grasp what is being suggested. Particularly if a completely new idea is being discussed it is likely to be misheard. This is not deliberate perversity but because we naturally gather ideas together in a network of interrelated themes. Therefore if the individual has not thought about the subject before there is no existing network into which it can be slotted, and it can be linked with the wrong pattern. This is why 'we hear what we want to hear', and leaders need to make allowances for it by giving people time and opportunity to grasp fresh ideas. Communication which is appropriate and reinforced is particularly important for this. Helping people to experience 'safe' examples in the life of another church is one of the best methods of communication, for many people find words less easily grasped than a practical example.

Drive. Every change brings out both positive and negative forces. The amount of force remaining when the negative force has been subtracted from the positive can be summed up as *drive* – the energy available to make a change happen. Where the positive forces of discontent and vision are stronger than the negative forces of fear then change will happen. Where the negative is stronger then change will be thwarted, however many resolutions are passed by committees. Indeed many people will be happy to vote for the most outrageous schemes, secure in the knowledge that they will never happen. Further where resources are not available then change will not occur – decisions will be made but subsequently found to be impracticable. Where there is an equality of forces an uneasy balance results which is often destructive of trust and enables nothing to be achieved. Kurt Lewin proposed his 'force field theory' which held that 'every institution is held in a state of equilibrium through the operation of positive and negative forces which counterbalance each other'. While this may be unduly pessimistic, and only descriptive of a 5,5 situation, it is true of many churches as well as other human groupings.

The amount of drive available can be increased by 'operating in the negative force field'. It is comparatively easy to reinforce the positive by explaining over and over again why a change would be beneficial. It is more difficult, but more worthwhile, to deal with the people who feel threatened and confused and those who have misheard from the start. Merely restating the positive means that people dig their heels in more firmly and their negative feelings are reinforced. By personal visits, by careful explanations which speak plainly of the difficulties of the suggestions as well as the benefits, and by giving a platform to the gainsayers, these forces can be met and helped to a more constructive frame of mind. They may not come to agree with the change but they cannot claim to have been disregarded. I have been to too many churches where this has not been done. Those advocating change become more and more shrill and insistent, while the others settle down into a 'they shall not pass' attitude. Trench warfare ensues with each reinforcing their position by any means possible. It does not make for a healthy Body of Christ.

Helping change to happen

There are certain ways in which it is possible to help people to understand the need for change, to accept and then implement it. These are not manipulative tricks but ways of encouraging a real consideration of what is proposed and enabling a sensible decision to be made.

Courtesy. Any suggestion that people are being railroaded by a 'hard sell' technique is certain to be counter-productive. People should be treated as adults or they will act as children. It may be possible to get a favourable vote at a meeting by political manoeuvring or over-persuasive presentations, but in the long run the scheme will founder because of the mistrust that has been engendered. In all probability it will be sabotaged by lethargy or hidden opposition. Leaders who are aware that they can easily carry a meeting by the force of their personality, or because they are trusted by the people, need to be wary in case they abuse that position.

It is also failing to treat people as adults to expect them to give a response on the spot to a scheme which has only just been sprung on them at that meeting. Except in extreme emergency people need time to adjust to a new idea, to talk about it informally, and to think more deeply about the problem it seeks to solve.

For those presenting a proposal to claim without qualification that it is the will of God puts any who have doubts into a difficult situation. Either they will keep silent for fear of appearing 'unspiritual' or they will react negatively and irrationally to what seems to them to be a claim to infallibility. If the decision is to be made by a body of people the proponents might be wiser to pray that the Spirit of truth would lead them collectively into all truth, rather than playing the 'Holy Spirit trump-card' which can appear to stifle further discussion. The suggestion should be able to stand up on its own arguments.

In the same way the leaders should seek not to become too personally involved. If they imply that a vote against a suggestion is also a vote of no confidence in their own leadership, people become unclear what they are deciding. They may agree with a proposal made in this way out of loyalty and against their own judgement, and the church come to regret it. Only in extreme cases should an issue end with an 'agree or we resign' vote, for it can appear to be blackmail by the leadership.

Experiment. The use of the 'experimental period' is of value. Many are hesitant to approve what they have never seen in action. It is sensible to test-drive a car before buying it. To suggest trying something out for a period indicates that the leadership is prepared to change its mind if the experiment is unsuccessful: they recognise that there is no guarantee of success; that the inevitable complications which will happen in practice will be taken into account; that those with contrary views realise that the final decision is not yet made; and that alterations to the scheme are possible when the experiment comes to be reviewed. However, an experimental period has to be fair to what is proposed. One church decided to try a new form of liturgy on the *fifth* Sunday of the month for a year. Not surprisingly they decided after the year was past that the old was better. Any experiment has to have fair trial and a proper review before a final decision is made. There are dangers in the use of this method. As mentioned before, difficulties caused by a change tend to surface before the benefits are felt. Further the lapse of time can lead to lobbying by those who are disgruntled, and a hardening of positions. However in many cases trying something for a 'test period' is good leadership.

Persuasion. Research by Rogers and Shoemaker showed that people accepted change at different rates. They distinguished five groups of people.

(a) Innovators. These like change and often initiate it.[6] They are regarded warily by those who are more cautious, and there is an ever-present danger that their proposal will become 'X's idea', and the whole issue becomes personalised.[7]

(b) Early Adopters. These form the first group to be persuaded of the rightness of a planned change. They are often people of weight in the community and are respected for their judgement. While the Innovators are suspected for their over-enthusiastic approach, the Early Adopters are listened to and heeded. Therefore if this group is persuaded of the rightness of a suggestion, the wise Innovator sits back and lets them do the persuading. As an Anglican vicar said, 'Win the key old ladies, set them loose to "gossip the good news of what's going on" and you're home and dry.'[8]

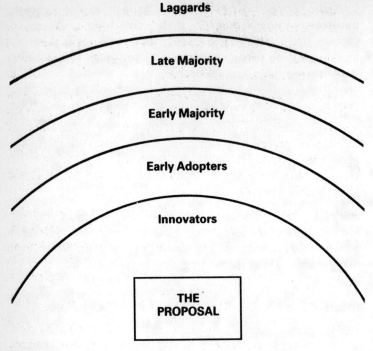

Fig. 9

(c) Early Majority. At this stage the bulk of the people involved are persuaded by the suggestion. These merge with:

(d) Late Majority. These comprise more cautious individuals who are less easily caught up by the movement of support.

(e) Laggards. These are those who stay at the 0,0 position in Figure 8. They are unlikely to be persuaded, though they may acquiesce if they see that there is a large majority for the suggestion. It could be that a trial of strength is attempted: 'If you agree to this I am leaving the church.' A wise leader always accepts resignations and rejects attempted blackmail of this kind. The pastor's heart is torn but the good of the whole cannot be held back because of

the obstinacy of a few vocal individuals. Sustained opposition of this kind can be one of the hardest times in a
person's ministry, for often it becomes personalised and
vitriolic, as John experienced when Diotrephes was
'gossiping maliciously about us'.[9]

There is always a danger that people will feel over-persuaded
if it is not recognised that to move in a certain direction means
leaving behind some things which are held dear. The familiar
has its own attraction, even if it is shabby, and people relinquish
it with reluctance. The innovator is shrewd if he is prepared to
recognise this sense of loss, even if he does not share it, and
allow time for people to come to terms with it.

Setting the boundaries of change. It may be right to declare that
there is a limit on the amount of change which is to be expected.
Often people are more opposed to what they think is coming
next than to the proposal before them. They mutter about the
thin end of the wedge. It may be right to say that there is no
wedge. If, however, the suggestion is part of a continuing process of change, it would be dishonest not to reveal it.

Consultation. Consulting others is important. But not all decisions should be thrown open to everyone – some are too petty
and would waste the time of the congregation, while others
involve confidentiality and should be restricted. But, as a
general rule, the more people are involved in a decision the
more they will support its implementation. This takes time,
especially in a large church. It means helping the congregation
to climb from the 0,0 position by explaining carefully what the
problem is, and then proposing the solution. Major decisions
– a building programme, a mission – can take many months of
consultation.[10] It is time well spent – up to a point.

That point is reached when the decision-making body tries
to avoid making a difficult decision by endless consultation
'until we all come to a common mind'. Some churches try to
consult everyone about everything. Indeed in many Baptist
churches this is written into the constitution. But there are
dangers. Consultation should be as widespread as is necessary,

but no more. It should never be seen as a device whereby the PCC or other body is absolved of the responsibility of making their own decision under God and living with the consequences. The result of such consultation should be seen as merely one factor to take into account in reaching a decision. The decision-makers need to set themselves a deadline after which they will stop consulting and make the decision.[11]

A consultation process will usually come to the conclusion that not everyone in the congregation is agreed on the proposals. The tendency of the decision-makers is to compromise, because they do not want to hurt anyone. This may be the right solution, but not necessarily so. The end can be a mishmash which satisfies no one and hampers the mission of God in the community. For example, if you give everyone the style of worship they want, you will end up with a multiplicity of services. This will encourage a supermarket church where each takes off the shelves what they want rather than what God wishes for them.

The rule book. Virtually all churches have written or unwritten rules, especially where the handling of money is concerned. It is important that such rules are kept when new ideas are being decided upon or there is the possibility that someone will pipe up 'On a point of order, Mr Chairman'. The Christian leader should have a good knowledge of the rules which govern the church and of normal practice for meetings – remembering that to some members of your meeting the ordering of business is second nature.

Willingness to change the plan. While the various elements of presentation, consultation, decision-making and implementation are happening the world is changing. There are great dangers in immutable five-year plans because the world is a different place at the end of the five years, and one which cannot be foreseen. Plans should always be sufficiently flexible to adapt to changed circumstances. It is noticeable that in industry the life of a product, or of a particular method of working, is getting shorter. A generation ago a particular brand of refrigerator would sell for 10 years or more: now it is becoming obsolete after two. In working through the process of change, it should always be made clear that revision may be necessary in the light of changed circumstances. People will find this reassuring: they rightly dislike being put on tramlines that carry them willy-nilly on a certain track into the future.

Not only is the world changing as time passes: so is the church and its needs. For example, it is noticeable that churches will swing from a small groups structure to a more centralised one, and back again. This apparent inconsistency shows an ability to react to where people are at any moment.[12] An over-tight plan can stifle this natural need for variety.

To be a leader in an organisation undergoing major change can never be a comfortable position. Certain defensive reactions can be seen in leaders who are finding the going hard. Each brings forth a predictable counter-response from the congregation.

LEADER	CONGREGATION
Withdraws from the battle and abdicates responsibility	Feeling bereft of leadership, they flounder. Alternative leadership may emerge
Becomes inflexible and refuses to listen to the opinions of others	Angry because their opinions are not valued
Loses the overall vision in the mass of detailed decision-making	Confused, because they forget why the changes are necessary
Becomes angry with those who disagree	Almost always counter-productive, for it personalises the issues
Becomes too wedded to one particular way forward	Obstinacy is often met with obstinacy

LEADER	CONGREGATION
Switches leadership styles – usually becoming either more authoritarian or wheedling	Any attempt to 'pull rank' or elicit sympathy is deeply resented

Conclusion

The process of introducing change can be summarised in the diagram (Fig. 10). It may be helpful to check this against any recent change that has taken place in your church or other organisation that you know well.

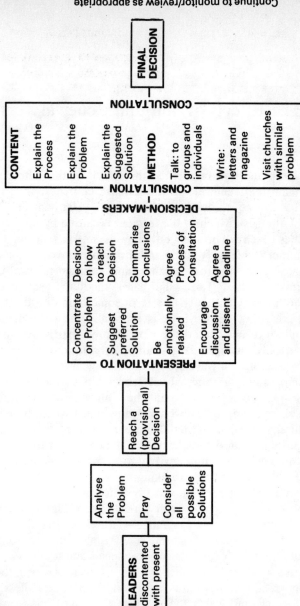

Continue to monitor/review as appropriate

In some contexts LEADERS and DECISION-MAKERS may be one group

Fig. 10

7

The Effects of Spiritual Renewal

In 1985 Josephine Bax researched the effects of the different kinds of 'spiritual renewal' on the English churches. In *The Good Wine* she concludes that 'there is a lay ferment and a management crisis'. Much of the ferment is caused by the new spiritualities which are bringing both new life and new problems into the hitherto relatively placid and shrinking pool of national churchmanship. People may brush against spiritual renewal in many forms: *cursillos*,[1] Taizé pilgrimages, meditation seminars all give both clergy and laity a taste of something outside the normal parish diet. However it is especially the charismatic movement which has caused the most turmoil, partly because it is numerically much the largest and partly because its questionings of established ways are the most radical.

It is impossible to think about leadership in the current church without taking into account these movements for spiritual awakening. Indeed one wonders how much would be left of the church in England if there had not been such quickenings of the Spirit. It is hard to believe that the church of the early 1960s could have survived in any real form without these injections of spirituality and new thinking.

But they have not been universally welcomed. A layperson comes back from a *cursillo* with a new love of Jesus and a longing to witness to him: her Anglo-Catholic church finds it difficult to contain her enthusiasm. A charismatic prayer group operates in the parish and talks of prophecies and tongues and healings in a way which mystifies and alarms the majority of the congregation. A person returns from Taizé humming endlessly repetitive songs and wants to introduce them into the parish

Eucharist, while another comes back from a meditation weekend and wishes to have little but profound silence.

Although there have been many disappointments and not a few divisions, these movements for renewal have now become a familiar part of the scene. There are very few churches which have not been affected in some way, even if it be only to act as a refuge from the church up the road.

It may seem almost blasphemous to examine the results of these workings of the Holy Spirit, but there are certain common factors and lessons to be learned. There is no blueprint, for the 'Spirit bloweth where it listeth' and there must be no attempt to copy a paradigm and hope that the Holy Spirit will be bound by it. However, ours is a God of order, as Paul reminded the tumultuous church at Corinth,[2] and therefore it is not surprising that we can map the wind of the Spirit in the same way as the meteorologist can put arrows on his weather charts. The limited success of the weatherman with all his computers should, however, give us a becoming humility.

It seems possible to recognise four stages in the progress of a church into renewal. There is much overlapping between the stages, and churches experience sudden leaps forward or 'plateaux' of apparent stagnation, but the overall pattern is discernible.

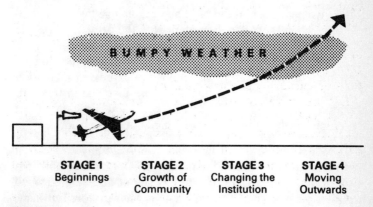

STAGE 1 Beginnings	**STAGE 2** Growth of Community	**STAGE 3** Changing the Institution	**STAGE 4** Moving Outwards

Fig. 11

Stage 1. The beginnings of renewal

Churches which have experienced renewal often find two complementary factors at work, prayer and spiritual hunger. Indeed they belong together. It is hardly coincidental that it was after Christ had prayed that the disciples came to him and expressed their own spiritual hunger: 'Lord, teach us to pray.'[3] Where a church appears to be sunk in apathy it is possible to pray spiritual hunger into it in the same way that blowing on apparently dead embers often breathes a fire into flame. When a minister complains that there is no life in a church it is permissible to ask if he has tried sustained, persevering, believing prayer. The clergyman who complained to his bishop about the lack of life in his parish received the reply, 'What do you think I put you there for if it was not to make it live?'

The attitude of the leadership towards renewal is crucial. It may be that the leaders are personally involved in renewal. If so, the danger is that they rush ahead and leave behind the bulk of the congregation. Renewal then becomes limited to 'those people' who are in that prayer group, have been to Taizé, and so on. There are certain principles which such leaders need to bear in mind:

(1) As we have seen in the last chapter, change becomes possible only when there is a discontent with the present. If people are basically satisfied with their spiritual life they will look askance at any suggestion that it ought to be improved. Indeed they will indignantly refute any implied or expressed suggestion that they are worse Christians than those involved in renewal. Spiritual hunger is not engendered by constant castigation from the pulpit but by prayer and teaching about wider horizons.

(2) Leaders should do all they can to prevent any implication that some are 'first-class Christians', while others are not. It is wiser – and more scriptural – to talk about all being engaged in a pilgrimage as they explore what God has in store for them. St John's, Harborne called its midweek meeting 'Open to God',

which gave succinctly the attitude of adventurous expectancy as they waited to see what God would do. Nothing should be said or implied which denigrates any previous Christian knowledge or experience. Courtesy and love demand it. If someone has only a 'Sunday school faith' it is a foundation on which to build not an erection to be demolished. Hence the avoidance of labels, 'in-language', cliques is essential.[4] The leader is the one to whom all will look; if he or she spends excessive time with the people in renewal and ignores the rest there will be a justifiable annoyance. When I was in this position myself I felt it right to spend twice as much time with the people who were not involved with renewal as those who were.

(3) At this stage the Holy Spirit often uses outside agencies. A book is read and opens up new possibilities, a conference is attended that reveals new life elsewhere, people from another church join the congregation and talk of the growth, excitement and movement that they enjoyed before.

(4) There is a constant temptation for the leadership to forget the inward and spiritual, and concentrate on the outward and visible. To introduce 'spiritual songs', every-member ministry, participative worship is *not* to introduce renewal. We always seek to avoid the personal pain of encountering God. Churches have put on the trappings of renewal without experiencing the heart-changing filling of the Holy Spirit. There always has to be a deep personal repentance and a risk-taking commitment to follow God wherever he may lead. Leaders need to be always trying to detect the ways in which God is being avoided. Probably the most usual is given in Canon Harry Sutton's dictum: 'The thing that stands between most Christians and their God is their work for God.'

(5) It is easy, in the excitement of a new affection, to lose sight of the ordinary and everyday. Those in love are normally useless around the house. The wise leader will encourage those engaged in renewal to be involved in the church with the 'chores

of grace' and outside the church in caring for the community and working effectively at their jobs.

(6) It is easy to forget that the reason why individuals are being renewed is that they may serve others. Renewal can become self-serving: groups turn inwards, churches concentrate on healing themselves, individuals become preoccupied with their own needs. It loses its way and the joy disappears. There is a danger of nostalgia and a hope that by doing the same things in the same surroundings the excitement can be recaptured. Often it is precisely because people are doing the same things that the enthusiasm has vanished – God has moved on. Good shepherds do not let a flock feed only on one pasture.

(7) Gavin Reid says: 'God always has an agenda which is a little bit different from our own.' It is too easy to have a mental blueprint of the way in which we expect renewal to happen. We may even encapsulate it on paper, and produce a plan for renewal. It is highly unlikely that God has exactly that pattern for the church. One disconcerting factor is the way in which God uses all the different forms of renewal. They flow together. One person makes their *cursillo* and comes back 'filled with the Spirit', while another who has gained much from the charismatic movement is led into meditation and the use of silence.

(8) It is so easy to forget the amount of time which it all takes. In my experience churches take between 2 and 10 years for renewal to become a normal part of congregational life: usually it tends towards the longer period. Leaders easily become impatient and try to prompt the Holy Spirit; they become despondent and even leave their church for other orchards which appear to have more fruit. It may be useful to remember that from inception to completion an oil tanker takes 8 years, a nuclear power station 15 and a Channel Tunnel nearly 190. Spiritual temples are seldom built overnight. We need *architectoi*[5] – master builders who can lay a sound foundation, not jerry builders who construct spiritual shanty-towns on sand.

Another situation may have leaders who are not personally

involved with the various forms of renewal, yet find people in their churches who are influenced by them and are pushing the leaders to 'do something about it'. This can lead to a defensive leadership and a frustrated laity.

It is often true that the people involved are some of the most faithful and regular members of the congregation. They often have the widest vision and are prepared to work to make it happen. There is all the more reason therefore for there to be harmony between them and the church leadership, and it is a foolish leader who does not consider this carefully.

It is difficult to enter into something with which one is personally unsympathetic. Yet if God has been working in this way, we cannot turn it down and merely say that it is 'un-Anglican', 'divisive', 'fundamentalist', 'unevangelical' or whatever our own theological swearwords are. Any true spiritual leader has to seek God wherever he may be found, remembering the awful example of the Pharisees who could not see the reality of the God who was daily before their eyes.

First the leadership needs to be aware of the nature of the other person's enthusiasm. It is too easy to mentally label people as 'charismatic', 'catholic', 'evangelical', and look for the responses you expect. The experience may be very new to them and they will often be inarticulate and almost certainly theologically imprecise. Sometimes it means so much that they can hardly talk about it. The leaders will need pastoral skill not merely to hear but to understand. And we need always to be asking ourselves: 'What is God trying to teach me through this person?'

Secondly there should be an affirmation of the other person's experience. It may be something which is unappealing or even distasteful to us, but its significance to the other is great and we should not attempt to 'talk them out of it'. We will not succeed if we try and it will only drive them into a bewildered silence. It is like talking to someone who is in love, and it is a silly parent who criticises their child's sweetheart.

Thirdly there should be an attempt to integrate this into the life of the church. It is better to have an official prayer meeting or 'fourth day' group for *cursillistas* than that people should gather semi-secretly. These people wish to be close to God and we should enable them to fulfil this and feed their experience into the wider life of the church, rather than allow them to feel misunderstood and unappreciated.

Stage 2. The growth of community

Those who are involved in renewal feel drawn to others to love and to share. I have never found a church where there is real renewal where there has not been a group meeting more or less regularly. Even a parish which had a strong emphasis on personal meditation had a series of meditation groups. Love is a sign of the genuineness of any spiritual awakening. *Agape* is the touchstone either to validate or to disprove any experience. This is not just an emotion, it is a caring for the other with the whole of our being in Christ.[6] This group life is a distinguishing factor of renewal. People gather into groups in order to:

(a) reinforce and explore further their experience of Christ
(b) learn more about the faith
(c) seek the way ahead
(d) receive support so they can act constructively outside the group, and
(e) pray together.

These aims are not always achieved, and help needs to be given in some cases.

The leadership of the church will need to be much involved at this stage. Whatever their personal opinion they will need to see that the groups are set up sensibly, give advice on handling pastoral problems, and help with publicity. However they would be wise not to jump into a position of automatic leadership. Often these are specifically *lay* initiatives, and they should not be stifled. The *episkope* role is essential here – to monitor and assist, rather than organise and control.

In particular the leaders will find they are having to take

risks. Lay initiatives mean that much new ground is broken and many mistakes are made. The leadership has to remember that the encouragement of lay ministry is one of the greatest tasks laid upon them, and must be prepared to bear with the rough edges for the sake of future growth. It is not always easy. Many ministers say that when renewal begins in a church everyone leans upon the minister, but after a couple of years they begin to try out their wings for themselves, and move from dependence to independence. It is said that children start the 'age of negativism' at 2 years old: Christian babies are not dissimilar. Hopefully babies grow through this phase into an adult relationship.

At this stage the main institutions of the church are not threatened. People will need to be informed of what is happening to avoid any idea of the creation of a new secret society but they themselves can come along to church on a Sunday or to the normal organisations of the church, and not be much affected. The life of the groups may be close and valuable to those who attend, but they make little impact on the church as a whole. Indeed it may be right deliberately to allay suspicion by encouraging the groups to undertake tasks around the church so that people can see they are ordinary and sensible people, to be welcomed rather than treated with suspicion.

There is usually a growing circle of people involved with renewal. Some may lose their first enthusiasm, but others will join and the group life quickly becomes part of the furniture of the church. People cease to wonder at it, or be worried by it, especially if it has been publicised carefully from the start. However there are some people who need careful handling. The love that is in the church will attract many, not all of whom are helpful. Among them are the mentally disturbed and socially inadequate; these should be welcomed in the name of Christ for there are few other places where they can receive friendship and healing within a community. There are the spiritual gad-flies, those self-appointed 'messengers of the Lord' who always have a 'word' for the leaders of a church (usually condemnatory). They should be treated with extreme caution: if God has a word for a church he usually tells the leaders directly.[7] There are the exhibitionists who parade their hurts as though they were campaign medals, and who always look for 'ministry' or 'counselling', who should be helped to look away from themselves to the distresses of others. But there are many others who come: some wistfully seeking something greater from life, some conscious of their need for the 'peace which transcends all understanding', some desperate for healing from personal failure and shame. Each in their own way finds 'abundant life' in Christ and are added to the fellowship, and there is rejoicing in heaven itself.

In order to encourage the growth of spiritual renewal in the church it is usual for various events to be organised. Charismatic churches frequently run a series of 'Saints Alive!' groups.[8] Others will take folk to *cursillos*, to Taizé, or on retreats. The intention should not be for others to have an identical experience. That is impossible. It is to enable other people to see what has been so liberating for the original group, and to allow them to come to their own conclusions and experience the work of the Holy Spirit in their own way.

Often this is called the 'Springtime in the Church'.[9] People are excited by the reality of God in a way which is exhilarating and enlivening. They begin to think new thoughts and dream new dreams:

> then was our mouth filled with laughter
> and our tongue with singing.
>
> (Ps. 126:2)

Those who have the privilege of leading a church through this period of its life often look back on it as a time of great personal happiness and growth. It is an atmosphere reflected in the early chapters of Acts, when almost anything seemed possible, and the church had not yet undergone hard persecution from without or sharp differences within. It is the time when God strengthens and encourages Christians, shows them what true Christianity really is and enables them to learn to live in trust.

Faithful people find a new meaning to their faith, and non-Christians find God for themselves.

It is not a stage to be rushed for the next stage is not so easy. Three or four years is not unusual, and many churches have found that the roots of renewal are not firm enough to withstand the gales of stage 3 when they have moved forward too soon. But progress there has to be if the church is to be faithful to God. He does not merely want a few groups of joyful, praying Christians, he wants churches renewed in the Spirit, and able to serve the world he created and for which he died.

Stage 3. Changing the institution

Up to this point the ordinary life of the church has gone on largely unperturbed. There may have been minor changes. One vicar, who picturesquely described his personal renewal as 'when I got the wind', had an unsolicited testimony from his churchwarden: 'The vicar preaches different nowadays – he's got a sort of authority he didn't have before.' There may be a difference in the way in which church committees are conducted, and there will be a greater emphasis on prayer and Bible and sacrament. But there have been few deep difficulties.

Stage 3 is when the normal life of the church begins to be affected. It shows itself when the worship on Sunday begins to alter, when the organisations begin to be adversely affected by the number of people in house groups, when the atmosphere of the church changes.

Worship is the usual problem area. Renewal of any kind tends to lead to services which are both more objective and God-centred, and also more directly engage the members of the congregation. One church I attended had a period of guided meditation as a considerable part of their morning worship, led by members of the meditation group with what seemed to me great sensitivity. But it was clear that the congregation was fiercely divided for or against this departure from the norm, some welcoming the quiet and prayerfulness, while others felt desperately uncomfortable: 'like having Remembrance Sunday every week' as someone said. This unease is compounded by the differences which renewal down the ages has brought to the music of the church. The organ is no longer seen as the only possible instrument for 'sacred music', and robed choirs do not monopolise the singing.[10] The style of modern hymns, the lilt of Taizé chants, or the enthusiastic beat of charismatic songs do not always fit with a musical tradition which has great beauty but does not always encourage participation.

When modern liturgies are introduced at the same time the possibilities of an explosion are considerable. Sociological factors can come into play. This stage is usually a good deal less painful in UPA parishes, where participation and modern music is much more part of the culture than in churches inhabited by what has been called the 'chattering classes' who loudly articulate their grievances and know which strings to pull.[11] Rural churches are so diverse that it is impossible to generalise, though again it tends to be true that the 'higher' up the social scale the congregation is the more difficult this period of renewal becomes.

The way in which conflicts like these can be handled personally is dealt with in greater detail in Chapter 8, but the possibility of them must always be faced. The church scores low on the way in which it handles disagreements. Political adversaries can be extremely rude about each other's opinions and then have a friendly drink together, but churches seem to find it difficult to cultivate this forbearance. Change is a natural part of the work of God and Christian leadership cannot escape the need to introduce it sensibly and sensitively.

Leaders are wise to distinguish between the 'problems of life' and the 'problems of death'. The former should be welcomed. If the young Christians in the church are rather foolishly over-enthusiastic, then the leaders should rejoice as they give counsel. If a house group is becoming too independent, then rejoice as it is sorted out. But if the energies of the church are sucked into bemoaning dwindling congregations, or raising money from an ever smaller number of people, then these are the problems of death, and resurrection is the only answer.

Stage 3 is not all difficulty. Any perplexities should be seen as growing pains, for the whole church is now being affected by renewal, and people are becoming more aware of God. The vision now is for the whole church and not just for a small group of people. Dreams become possibilities, and possibilities become realities. The aircraft rises steadily through the clouds, despite the air pockets which cause an occasional lurch and sensations of unease in some of the passengers.

Stage 4. The church in renewal

The problems of stage 3 have been worked through, the joys of stage 2 have not been forgotten, and now the church has moved into a 'steady state', where renewal is normal and generally accepted. This does not mean that there are no problems, but they tend to be less personal and more subtle. It is at this stage that the church must discern the way of God, or consolidation can lead to slumber.

In some ways it is a dangerous time, just as the occupation of the Promised Land was potentially perilous for the Israelites. The temptations are the same:

(1) 'Jeshurun grew fat and kicked . . . he abandoned the God who made him and rejected the Rock his Saviour.'[12] Christians are often better when they are journeying than after they have arrived. The pilgrimage must continue, though possibly in a different direction. Nearly always this is in some form of mission, as God makes use of the church he has forged.

(2) 'Be careful not to make a treaty with those who live in the land; for when they prostitute themselves to their gods and sacrifice to them, they will invite you and you will eat their sacrifices.'[13] The church which sees itself as having arrived will come to a *modus vivendi* with the community, not in a helpful

way from which both benefit, but in a way which smooths out the angularities of the Christian faith, and its challenge is lost in a sea of blandness. A church faithful in mission will want to get outside its buildings and its 'safety zone' and both learn from and evangelise the community.

(3) 'It is not because of your righteousness that the Lord your God is giving you this good land to possess.'[14] A static church, however outwardly 'successful', is always liable to let God slip into the background, and to claim that it was *our* leadership, *our* tenacity, *our* faith that brought us to this position. Pride is not only individual, it can be corporate. There is a false pride in our church as we thank God 'that we are not as other churches are'.

God does not renew a church just for its own good. By definition renewal is for the benefit of someone else. Churches should ultimately be serving their community and the world. In other words a church which has reached stage 4 needs, in the terms of Chapter 1, to turn over and become a 'flower-pot' church if it is to continue to grow and flourish. Up to stage 3 the church has probably not been a 'flower pot'. It has widened its base, established its group life and enlarged its leadership, but the 'lines of force' in the church are still internal. If it is called to concentrate on the mission of its members outside the life of the church, then there needs to be the change of attitude which the 'flower pot' requires.

This does not, of course, mean that the church should not engage in mission until stage 4 has been reached, but it does mean that once this stage is attained the energies of the church must quite deliberately be turned outwards. As part of this process leaders have to learn the art of diminishing in personal prominence and changing their style. Leadership needs to become more subtle. Once leaders were required to provide strong leadership. Now they are just as necessary but in a less conspicuous way. It is not easy to loosen one's hold on a church for which one has given some of the best years of one's ministry:

to say with John the Baptist, 'He must become greater: I must become less'[15] requires real humility and joy in the growth of others. Leaders may find themselves surprisingly free to travel and broaden their ministry. Several churches have experimented, not always successfully, with a rector who is the original leader and now has a ministry outside as well as within the church, and a vicar who cares for its everyday running.

It needs to be repeated again that these stages do not occur in the same way in every church, but approximate to what is frequently experienced. The parallel should not be taken too literally, but this pattern compares with the experience of the early church depicted in Acts:

Chapters 1 and 2	Stage 1:	the disciples are filled with the Holy Spirit and begin to gather together for prayer and learning
Chapters 3–5	Stage 2:	the group enlarges and 'difficult' people have to be confronted; conflict with the religious establishment begins
Chapters 6–8	Stage 3:	corporate problems emerge. The establishment becomes seriously worried and persecution begins in earnest
Chapters 8 onwards	Stage 4:	the church turns outwards in mission.

Acts 1–7 suggests a church where the dynamic is primarily internal. If opportunity presents itself the Gospel is preached and new people are welcomed, but there is little deliberate evangelism.

Acts 8 onwards describes a church dedicated to evangelism,

and consciously praying about its strategy for mission. It is a 'flower-pot' church where the leaders (to judge from the Epistles) see their work as being to ensure that the ministry of each individual is valued and used.

Conclusion

(1) If your church has experienced the beginnings of renewal in the lives of individuals, it is helpful to assess which of the different types of renewal have been the most fruitful.

(2) Which of the four stages of renewal does your church fit into most easily, and what is likely to happen next?

8

The Strains of Leadership

It would be foolish to suppose that the Christian leader is likely to escape various kinds of pressure. This chapter looks first at the ways in which conflict can be managed within the church, and secondly at the pressures a leader may encounter. This is not to insert a sour note into a book on leadership, but to be realistic.

Conflict and pressure are by no means always to be avoided. Conflict often leads to the exposure of truth and to progress; indeed it is likely that there will be very little movement unless there is some disagreement. Demands upon a leader are often a spur to action rather than a hindrance. The pressure of a deadline makes us get down to work; the pressure of people's needs makes us respond in love; the pressure of financial difficulties helps us to review what we are doing.

The handling of conflict

Any real growth brings pain; whether it is change brought about by spiritual renewal, an increase in numbers, the clearing out of the obsolescent, or any other reason, there will be the likelihood of tension. Any leader will have to come to terms with this from time to time, and should be able to do so constructively and without extreme personal pain.

This raises several questions. The main one concerns how people deal with dissension. But there are also important subsidiary questions about the ways in which a dispute may be handled.

Disputes have two levels. On the surface there is the cause of the disagreement. Under the surface there are the emotions which it has produced. Often there are the emotions which produced the conflict in the first place. Some differences produce little emotion and can be rationally discussed and decided. But where strong feelings interact with rational arguments, disputes can be protracted and difficult to manage.

A fierce disagreement can appear from an apparently clear sky when there has been a build-up of resentment about other matters. 'A great forest is set on fire by a small spark' (Jas. 3:5). Frequently a minor issue ignites an inferno. This is often the case when a power struggle is taking place. One parish I was in had a group of very influential people who questioned everything I proposed. I soon learnt that they were known locally as the 'Royal Family', were accustomed to run everything in the village and I was proving less amenable than they had hoped. Every trivial problem produced a prolonged dispute.

The issue may become increasingly personalised. A disagreement about, say, new lighting in the church, becomes a covert attack upon the way the leader is running the church. There are many examples in the gospels where the authorities came to Jesus with a difficult question, not in order to find an answer, but to have a pretext for a personal attack. Often to designate an idea as X's plan is enough to ensure its defeat, because X is not well liked.

The 'thin end of the wedge' argument often has emotional roots of this kind. It indicates a distrust of the leadership and what they are 'getting up to'. It is a suspicion which is born, not out of what has actually happened, but out of what is feared might be proposed in the future.

A controversy becomes increasingly over-simplified as it develops. People become unwilling to look at the complexities of the question, because to do so would blur the self-evident validity of their argument. They begin to talk in slogans. The words of Sam Goldwyn of Hollywood are worth remembering:

'To every complex question there is always a simple answer – and it is always wrong!'

We need to have an excuse before we allow our emotions to be put on public display. In Christian circles the excuses are often theological. When 'points of principle', backed by arguments from Scripture and tradition, emerge it often indicates a hardening of position.[1] If a leader, who may well be more theologically expert, then demolishes that argument, he may have done considerable harm because he has both failed to perceive the motivation behind the attack and crushed the person concerned.

Where there is a genuine point of principle involved, as when Paul confronted Peter with his duplicity and 'opposed him to his face',[2] it is important to draw out the real point of difference. It is then sometimes possible to discuss that in isolation without relating it to the emotionally charged subject at issue. One church had hired out its church hall to a class in transcendental meditation. Several members of the group had friends within the church. Questions were raised at the church council about the rightness of allowing church premises to be used in this way. Initially there was considerable anger from some because it appeared to attack their friends. However when it was agreed that no one knew enough about TM and it was important to discover the facts, the situation was defused and ultimately a calm decision was made.

When conflicts arise they can be personally devastating and bewildering, and bring much uncertainty to the church if they are not handled correctly. It is necessary to ask: Where is the best place for conflict to take place? When do we let it happen? What are the possible outcomes of conflict? How do we cope with it personally?

(1) *Where is the best place for conflict to happen?* The setting in which confrontation takes place has a marked effect on its course and eventual outcome. There is a world of difference between trying to talk a matter through with someone in their own living room and facing them at a church meeting with

half the congregation present. Wherever possible choose the surroundings which are most likely to lead to a resolution.

The atmosphere of the meeting is of the greatest importance: the image of people sitting on the same side of the table trying to work out the correct solution fosters cooperation, prayer and hope; the picture of a confrontation across the table hardens opinions. The wise leader seeks to lessen formality, lighten the atmosphere, and encourage every constructive comment.

(2) *When is the best time to face conflict?* It is not always possible to put off conflict until the 'best' time: it can suddenly face us in an enraged church member or a barbed motion proposed at a meeting. Where these sudden situations arise it is wise to seek for time – make an appointment to see the angry person, or postpone consideration of the motion until the next meeting. Normally there is a background of which the leader may be unaware, and a quiet talk in the privacy of a person's home may do much to defuse a situation.

However there are times when the leader should deliberately precipitate conflict. If he is conscious that there are undercurrents of dissatisfaction in the church it is often wise to bring them into the open where they can be looked at dispassionately.

Timing is important. Normally we postpone pain through procrastination. This is not always right. The most intractable situations are those where conflict has been avoided by various strategems over a long period but then comes suddenly to a head. Positions by this time have become so entrenched, and so much buried hurt surfaces, that the outlook is decidedly stormy. If the disagreements had been faced earlier it would have been healthier.

However, making every disagreement the subject of instant discussion is as futile in a church as in a marriage. There are many times when we have to accept other people, warts and all, and learn to laugh at their idiosyncracies and at our own overreactions. There are times when leaders need to practise the New Testament art of *epieikeia* – an almost untranslatable but vital quality: different versions suggest 'tolerance', 'magnanimity', 'gentleness', 'forbearance', 'longsuffering'.[3] There are some leaders who see conflict where there is none, and take every careless word too seriously.

(3) *The possible results of conflict.*[4] There are three possible scenarios:

(a) The conflict is understood to have been resolved by one side losing and the other winning. This may happen by referring the matter to higher authority – a bishop or other figure outside the particular church is often chosen. Similar appeals may be made to Scripture or some other authoritative writing such as canon law. But often situations find no such clearcut resolution – nor should they. Indeed one characteristic of strife is that one side or both try to force the disputed circumstances into some precedent. Very often, like Cinderella's slipper, precedent only fits the situation which gave rise to it in the first place.

(b) Conflict is avoided by each party withdrawing and pretending it is not happening. A lengthy stalemate ensues where each avoids the other and a show of indifference papers over the cracks. Churches can go on for years in such an unhealthy state. It may well have been such a division between two Christian leaders that Paul was seeking to bring into the open when he told Euodia and Syntyche to 'agree with each other in the Lord' (Phil. 4:2).

The division may well continue because no one is prepared to bring it to a head for fear of losing. Sometimes time itself brings a solution – someone moves away from the area or the cause of the dispute fades away: there is also the solution known to every Christian leader, 'where there's death, there's hope'. But side-stepping a difficulty is usually to avoid the possibility of growth. The situation grumbles on and on, poisoning relationships, with the constant likelihood of a major confrontation.

(c) The conflict is seen as capable of resolution. There can be either an agreement to disagree, while retaining a true respect for the other person, or a compromise solution can be hammered out. While there is nothing dishonourable in either of these positions there is another way which is best wherever possible: the view of neither party is accepted but a third option, preferable to the others, is found. This is often readily accepted since neither party to the dispute loses face by accepting it. Usually it surfaces because the dispute itself encourages lateral thinking which looks at the problem from different angles. Christ did this in the quarrel between James and John and the other disciples about places near him in his 'glory'. Christ showed that it was not as simple as they had supposed and that leadership in the Kingdom had the character of servanthood rather than lordship: he shifted the ground of the debate and in doing so solved it.[5] A leader will often find that he or she will be seeking such a solution when helping two people who are in disagreement. This can often be done by widening the vision. In a church where there was a considerable dispute about forms of service, with each stating his or her own preference, the debate was changed and eventually resolved, when it was suggested that the church should be considering those who are outside as well as those inside: this emphasis on mission altered the terms of the discussion and a solution was agreed which did not fit any of the previously expressed positions.

The lateral thinking which produces this 'alternative option' may also be needed by the leadership to look at the 'underside' of the dispute. They need to consider the personal motivations which may be causing the argument. In a debate on the rights and wrongs of the remarriage of divorcees in church, I noticed that all the people who were most vehemently opposed were themselves victims of broken homes. Their reasoning was dictated by their personal trauma. In other cases it may be sin which causes dissension, 'for from within, out of men's hearts come evil thoughts . . . malice, deceit . . . envy, slander, arrogance and folly'.[6] The experienced Christian leader has heard them all: indeed he knows of some within his own life.

Because disputes which are well handled bring issues into the open they can often be used to show us the real reasons for our words and actions. Anger is the servant of truth for it can unlock the door for us to say things which we feel are true, both about ourselves and others. While this can be negative it can also help us to realise why we reacted in the way we have. Indeed all leaders should be aware of those situations which lead to an inappropriate emotional response from themselves, or the sort of personalities in others which 'bring out the worst in us'. This in turn can lead to repentance and new beginnings. Such a recognition of the impact of emotion can make a resolution much more possible.

This third position, where resolution of the conflict is seen as possible, is the position of faith and of the 9,9 leader. It believes that all things are attainable under God, that repentance and a fresh start can happen, and that brothers and sisters can learn to live together in harmony. This more optimistic view also means that the Christian leader is not so ready to avoid conflict since so much can be learnt through its resolution. A period of renewal in the church may be a period when several conflicts emerge, but it may also be a sign, albeit a rather unnerving one, of the work of the Holy Spirit and the deepening of fellowship. It was the disagreement between the Gentile Christians and the 'Judaisers' which led, under God, to the acceptance by the church that the Gospel was for all the world, but it was far from pleasant for Paul and the others who endured the strain of it.

(4) *How do we cope with conflict?* Every leader should know ways which are personally helpful in dealing with tension. There are certain principles which may help in forming a policy for ourselves:

(a) Get the situation into perspective. Everything which stirs us deeply seems mountainous in the present and infinitely menacing in the future. In our blacker moments (usually as we toss from side to side at 4 am) there appears to be no possibility of light or redemption. Our prayers seem to be blighted by the circumstances and the problem looms behind all our thoughts. In these cases we need to be able to stand back. Each will choose the way which works for them. A *short* break is helpful to some (a long holiday is often spoilt by the brooding anticipation of what awaits us when we return). Others find extreme physical exertion useful, or a hobby where they can lose themselves for some hours. Others find going to a concert or a football match brings a more objective view. Some find prayer brings peace – though others find it impossible to get the trouble out of their minds and merely 'worry before God'.

(b) Find somebody who can help. To share a problem with someone who will listen and make few comments is valuable. In fact the verbalising of the difficulties will often suggest possible solutions without any recommendations from the other person. Usually the best person to go to is not someone who is too emotionally involved themselves, but a person who is neutral yet has been in similar positions. For this reason it is often unhelpful to go to our marriage partner or a party to the dispute who is 'on our side'. They will not be able to give the fresh unemotional thinking which is most needed.

(c) Trust in God. At times of stress some feel God to be very close, while others find he seems far away. These psychological reactions should not be taken to be spiritual truth. The fact is that he *is* with us, and our feelings do not matter. It can be helpful to think back to similar situations in the past when we emerged battered but unscathed through the aid of God.

(d) Make no sudden decisions. When we are in an emotional state it is unlikely that our judgement will be good. In particular, it is natural at such times to long to escape – 'O that I had the wings of a dove! I would fly away and be at rest . . . far from the tempest and storm'.[7] It is not sensible to make long-term decisions because of short-term difficulties.

(e) Some find it helpful to think back to past difficulties which are now no more than a memory. The children of Israel were continually told to look back to the Exodus and remind themselves 'if God got us out of that, he will surely get us out of this'.

The pressures of leadership

Once again it needs to be said that pressure is not something to be avoided. Bishop Michael Whinney likens the Christian leader to an elastic band. If there is not enough tension the band hangs limply around the parcel and it is no use. But if it has to be stretched so far that it snaps then that also is useless. It needs the right amount of tension to do its job.

But pressures can seem merely heavy weights which the leader is unable to master. Just as Adam's control over the animals was increased when he gave them names, so we can learn to come to terms with the forces which act upon us by examining and describing them.[8] The commonest pressures which confront a leader can be summarised in Figure 12.

God. It may seem strange to describe God as a pressure. But for a Christian he is a demand. This is not just the time which should be spent in prayer and study: it is the need for obedience, sometimes when our natural desire pulls the other way. All God's people have known the hound of heaven, who asks for trust, faith and obedience: 'If you love me you will obey what I command.' If we trust God, we will try to obey him, not out of compulsion but out of love. And the gentle pressure of God's love comes from the cross, and the vulnerability of the Trinity.

Where there is a pressure we may either try to ignore it or indulge it. We can try to evade God. He might interfere in our running of the church if we listen to him: he might ask us to

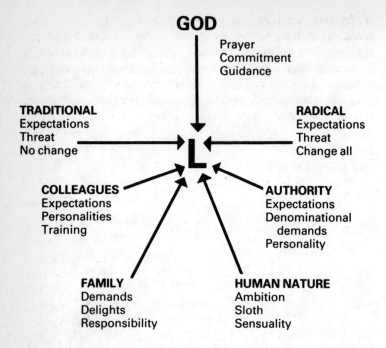

Fig. 12

change things in ways which seem hazardous and upsetting. Better not get too close. Alternatively we can spend too much time consciously with God, and ignore the other demands of ministry. It may be easier to pray for the sick than to pray with them, to pray for folk to become Christians than to witness to them, to pray for social justice than to visit those in prison. Christian leaders need to learn the balance that Moses had when he 'walked with God' – while he moved he remained with God. Wherever we go, whatever we do, we should practise the presence of God.

Tensions within the church. The diagram, for simplicity, shows only one tension in the church – that between the more traditional members and those who wish to move into new territory. It is by no means the only source of unease. There may well be a tug of war between those of different generations or social backgrounds or churchmanship. There may be strain between the newcomers and those who have been around a long time, between different organisations or those who attend one service rather than another. There is nothing unusual or shameful about this. The church should be a place where tensions are faced and transfigured through prayer and repentance into something infinitely varied and rich – the Kingdom of God. Nearly all the tensions above can be mirrored in the pages of the New Testament.

Facing these pulls from different directions the leader easily enters the 5,5 position of great discomfort. He or she is only able to react to the needs of others, and every initiative is quickly overwhelmed. Leaders feel torn apart between caring for the individual and caring for the whole church. It is no light burden. One feels that in that terrible list in 2 Corinthians 11 it was the 'daily pressure of my concern for all the churches' which was most onerous to Paul. To lead into a 9,9 position where the tensions are subsumed into a common vision requires skill and prayer. A 5,5 leader will tend to imagine that he or she is called to hold an even-handed balance between conflicting parties, favouring neither. But leadership tries to lead people onwards so that they accept and overcome the tensions rather than be possessed by them. To be at the 5,5 centre is a lonely experience: the leader satisfies no one. This is not suffering for the Gospel; it is a deficiency in leadership.

However it is too easy for a leader to be wholly identified with one side of the tension. In one church the minister was perceived to have 'no time for us old ones' and only to care for the 'incomers'. It was clear that the reason he spent more time with those who had newly arrived in the rapidly expanding village was that evangelistically they seemed much more responsive. It was suggested that the older members might be more accepting of his leadership (and more friendly towards the newcomers) if they could be included in the outreach wherever possible. In this way they would have a common goal, and be able to build upon the genuine wish of the older ones to see their church flourish. Subsequently the church stalwarts were engaged in baking cakes for 'meet your neighbour' parties, acting as guides for church 'open days', and looking after a crèche during services. Not only did it do a great deal to heal a rift in the community but it also brought many of the older people closer to their Lord.

Authority. Different forms of church government will have different bodies which exert this pressure. In a non-episcopal church it may be the congregation itself, a board of trustees or the kirk session. Sometimes the stress caused can be frighteningly powerful. I remember a minister from Chicago weeping because of what he saw as extreme pressure from the presbytery, and a Seventh Day Adventist minister who was in danger of losing his job because his theological position was changing. Others may feel that the bishop disapproves of them, or feel bound to obey every detail of canon law. Generally the closer the level of authority is to the local church the greater the leverage that can be exerted. When someone is answerable to their own congregation as in some church politics the pressure can be intense, and the temptation merely to react to the needs of the congregation correspondingly strong. The other extreme was voiced to me by a Roman Catholic priest on the west coast of Ireland who seemed to be breaking every rule in the book – 'Ah, the Pope is a long way away!'

The basis of the relationship between a leader and 'those set in authority over him' should be one of mutual trust. The bishop or other authority figure should be able to trust the leader concerned to get on with the job without interference: he in turn should be aware that this is the basis of the relationship. He should expect to be pulled up if he does what is wrong or stupid, but he should also expect personal support in times of difficulty and wise guidance in times of perplexity. Few denominations have evolved a suitable form of supervision. Either it is so close that it deprives the leader of initiative, or so distant that he is not properly supported. The present period of increasing pressure upon 'middle-management' means that this is a most serious lack which is leading to a high incidence of breakdown.

The team. Although we have discussed the concept of team leadership at some length in Chapter 3, it is worth recalling that colleagues can be a considerable pressure. There have been many leaders who have found that just adding to the numbers in leadership has not solved all problems – indeed may seem rather to have multiplied them. They rightly demand personal support, produce bright new ideas, react emotionally to your actions. It makes for a more complicated picture. It cannot be said that interactions between Christian leaders are easy. Poor relationships between incumbent and curates, or within an eldership team are common. While it is, of course, wise to work at these disagreements – often with the help of an outsider who is trusted by all – it is important not to spend too much time on them. I have found in many such situations that those involved can become obsessive and feel that God will not bless the church until relationships are put right: this in turn lays a greater burden of guilt and anger on those concerned. Fortunately our Lord seems to have taken a broader view: he was able to use the disciples and Paul and Barnabas despite their disputes.

Family. In the past, ministers and Christian leaders have been notorious for neglecting their families. They tend to be always around the house yet not available to the family, they work long hours, and the family shares the strains of the church without sharing the limited protection given to the leader by his or her status. 'Preacher's kids' have a reputation for wildness, and marriage partners have become 'spare curates' or have reacted violently against the church which seems to be the all-consuming love of their spouse's lives and which seems to exclude them. Divorce rates among Christian leaders, which used to be lower than the national average, are now about the same. In the United States it is said that if two ministers are married to each other the likelihood of divorce is over 90%.

It is in reaction against this history that many ministers and leaders now feel they need to protect their family from the difficulties of the church and spend much more time with them. Ministers often say, 'My family must be my first priority.' It is a dangerous statement for a Christian. Surely God and his will must be supreme. What has happened in the past is that leaders have sometimes mistaken their work for the church as being the will of God. The result has been overwork, 'burnout' and strained marriages. Too often the work of the church has been an escape from the demands of the family rather than a true work for the Lord. Our true priority should be to be doing what God wants at any particular moment – whether that means being with our family or being involved in the work of the church.

Each leader must work out with his or her family the right relationship with the church. The family should not be a warm, all-enveloping womb into which the leader retreats, and which becomes an excuse for poor leadership. Conversely he or she should support and encourage the family, both within the life of the church and beyond.

Self. The leader is a human being. Sometimes he or she forgets this. There are the usual desires, temptations and emotions. They are a powerful pull. The sins of the 'flesh, the world and the devil' have been with us since the dawn of human consciousness. But the leader may be more susceptible to them than others. He is essentially a 'front' man. This is by no means confined to the church. Charles Handy writes of the pressure upon the 'company man' to assume an identity with the supposed role: 'For many people, organisations seem to reek of this kind of private sin . . . they feel pushed to submerge their identity in the job, to argue cases of whose merit they are not convinced, give priority to rituals they know to be charades, be charming to those they despise, appear fierce when they feel sympathy, and act committed when unconvinced.'[9]

This pressure to provide an outward show leads to a lack of integrity, until the person becomes literally 'double-minded': part of him acts out the 'church' role and part is in rebellion against the requirement to fulfil this first role. Leaders can have a secret life, which they keep away from the God-centred part. This lack of wholeness quickly leads to a lack of holiness.

The need for an outward 'performance' leads to another danger for leaders. Because their work is never-ending, they feel a pressure to work very long hours.[10] But the quality of work is not always high. There can be a failure to concentrate on the task in hand which leads to an efficiency of 40% rather than one of 80% or higher. This means that not much is achieved despite the time consumed. Many leaders have been profoundly grateful for help in ordering their use of time. The courses available are often business-orientated, but it can be some relief to know that these pressures and temptations are not solely the blight of the Christian ministry.

Culture. The pressures we have described above are fairly easily named, and for that reason more readily faced and dealt with. They can be put on a diagram. But the surrounding culture is like the paper the diagram is printed on. It is the air we breathe, the climate we take for granted, the unexamined axiom of our life. Whether it is described as 'secularisation', 'scientism' or 'materialism' is immaterial. The prophetic voice of the church needs to examine again the foundations of our society, which are ever more complex, all-pervading, and difficult to resist. The work of Lesslie Newbigin in *Foolishness to the Greeks*[11] is of this kind, for he looked with fresh eyes at the culture of western civilisation as he returned to Europe after many years in India. This has to be a continuing work for Christian sociologists, anthropologists and theologians, but above all for prophets. The Old Testament prophets called into question the basis of their society; and the Christian church must do much more than mouth fashionable jargon and call it prophecy.

The Christian leader needs to be aware of the issues involved in this debate, for it shows him the variety of ways in which he is personally influenced, and how the mind-set of the people to whom he ministers is formed.

Conclusion

Charles Handy lists ten signs of stress: it is helpful to see how far they represent one's own behaviour.

(1) Polarise: it is easier to 'stand on principle' and decide between supposed black and white than deal with complexities.
(2) Shorten time-horizons: put off the long-term decisions.
(3) Search for routines: avoid having to make a decision by trying to fit the new situation into one which happened before.
(4) Delight in trivia: solve the easy problems.
(5) React rather than proact: after all to proact merely adds to what needs to be done.
(6) Flare up: emotional release becomes a safety valve.
(7) Withdraw: escape either physically or emotionally – 'none of it matters anyway'.
(8) Hammer away: work harder and try to get on top of the task.
(9) Escape into excess: self-indulgent behaviour patterns, 'I am working so hard I owe it to myself to relax', escape into drugs, sex, overeating, greed.
(10) Breakdown: the body or mind or spirit give up.

Management of time is important for any leader. Partly it is a matter of self-motivation. This is built upon a disciplined time with God.

General guidelines

(1) Tackle the tough questions first – the rest will seem easy afterwards.
(2) School oneself to think with concentration about a problem.
(3) Avoid crisis-management by planning time into your diary which gives you time to plan.

(4) Minimise interruptions when planning.

(5) Procrastination makes problems loom larger because guilt intrudes.

(6) The prayer attributed to Sir Francis Drake:

> Lord God, when you call your servants to endeavour any great matter, grant us also to know that it is not the beginning, but the continuing of the same, *until it be thoroughly finished*, which yields the true glory: through him, who for the finishing of your work, laid down his life for us, our Redeemer, Jesus Christ.

9

The Joys of Ministry

I remember once talking to Sister Doreen Gemmell of the Church Army. Her cancer-shrunken body seemed to be very frail and old. But she was overjoyed to have a new challenge. Here in the hospice with her were people who needed the Gospel. Her last months of life were given to ministry.

God does not leave his people to rust out. A businessman or a secretary will probably reach as high as they are going to get in their careers by the time they are in their early forties. The Christian leader is always faced by new ventures to try and new conundrums to answer. It is never a question of just coasting down to retirement; there are always fresh things to be learnt and the way of holiness to be attained. If Abraham could receive the covenant of God at 99, few of us need expect to live to be useless. Many new Christian initiatives have been taken by people who are comparatively elderly.[1]

One reason for this continuously developing ministry is that we play many roles in ministry: pastor, president, encourager, evangelist, counsellor, leader. The uppermost roles in our ministry may shift during our lifetime, so that one may be more prominent at one stage of our life than at another, but the result is the same – a varied and exciting ministry. Is it for this reason that clergy have a longer life expectancy than any other profession and that the vicarages and manses of Britain have produced such an abundance of gifted and talented children?

Thus there is a generally high level of job satisfaction among stipendiary ministers. A recent Gallup survey of Church of England clergymen showed that most were well satisfied with their job, and that those working in the highly stressful UPA areas had an even higher rate of job satisfaction than the rest.[2] 75% of clergy would 'very strongly' or 'quite strongly' encourage others to be ordained.

It seems clear that for most of those called to be leaders in the church, whether lay or clergy, their work provides an often exacting but always interesting environment. Creative and personal skills are demanded, and it requires constant thought and planning if the ministry is to be effective.

However it has to be accepted that the number of different roles which a leader plays can produce 'role overload'. This occurs when 'a person faces too many separate roles or too great a variety of expectations. The person is unable to meet all expectations satisfactorily and some must be neglected in order to satisfy others. This leads to a conflict of priority.'[3] Most leaders will recognise themselves in this description, with a multiplicity of roles to be played and insufficient time or flexibility to achieve all they would wish.

This profusion of functions leads to 'role conflict' where there are contradictory expectations coming from different directions. A study of the American restaurant industry showed that waitresses often cried. They found the job very stressful because there was constant friction between their role with the customers, who wanted their food as quickly as possible, and their role with the chefs who could not produce the food soon enough to keep the customers happy. Leaders in the church have role conflicts which are inherent in their ministry. In Chapter 2 we examined the discord which exists between the role of carer of the individual and that of carer of the whole church. But there are many others. For some the conflict between keeping the organisation moving ahead and at the same time evangelising those outside the church is acute. For others, the need to be steward of what is best in the past is in tension with their wish to be a shepherd leading the congregation to new pastures. Role conflict always induces feelings of guilt, which are hard to handle. It may be that the surprising finding of the Gallup poll about the greater job satisfaction of clergy in UPAs stems from the very pressures in which they minister. There are so many obviously good things which need to be done that those clergy may have less role conflict.

The rewards of ministry

For the true leader the only real reward must be to hear the Master's 'Well done, good and faithful servant'. Nevertheless it is foolish to deny that there are other satisfactions which come from this ministry.

Some are illegitimate gratifications. Christ castigated the Pharisees for their love of the trappings of leadership. The 'most important seats in the synagogues', the 'greetings in the marketplace' indicated their superiority to the rest of humanity. 'They were confident of their own righteousness and looked down on everybody else.' Whether it be an excessive concern with the details of liturgical robes or a delight in the honorific titles which have proliferated in the church, the modern Pharisee can be uncomfortably close to the surface in all of us who are leaders. Twentieth-century ecclesiastics, of all denominations, show the same 'yeast of the Pharisees, which is hypocrisy'. It works inwardly, subtly, destructively, changing the moral character of the leader until there is nothing left except outward show and inward corruption.[4] The Roman Catholic writer Margaret Hebblethwaite sees it as the prime hindrance to mission:

> The clericalist mentality is poison to the evangelising work of the church. It saps the spontaneous initiatives in ordinary Christians, and undermines their confidence. It undervalues the ministerial value of the real, earthy work of feeding the hungry, housing the stranger, healing the sick. It heaps honours on religious authorities with no regard to the teaching of Jesus: 'not so with you; rather let the greatest among you become as the youngest, and the leader as one who serves' (Luke 22:26). And it results in internal church conflicts that divert energy from our mission to the world. The laity are at least as guilty as the clergy in perpetuating this clericalist mentality.[5]

This true hypocrisy should be distinguished from the effect of the grace of God within the leader which others can see. Sometimes he is all too painfully aware of the discordance between this and what he knows of his own heart. Bonhoeffer in his prison put it most movingly:

Who am I? They often tell me
I would step from my cell's confinement
calmly, cheerfully, firmly,
like a squire from his country house.
Who am I? They often tell me
I would talk to my warders
freely and friendly and clearly
as though it were mine to command . . .

Am I then really all that which other men tell of?
Or am I only what I myself know of myself,
restless and longing and sick, like a bird in a cage,
struggling for breath, as though hands were compressing my throat,
thirsting for words of kindness, for neighbourliness . . .

Who am I? This or the other?
Am I one person today, and tomorrow another?
Am I both at once? A hypocrite before others,
and before myself a contemptibly woebegone weakling? . . .
Who am I? They mock me, these lonely questions of mine,
Whoever I am, thou knowest, O God, I am thine.[6]

In fact Bonhoeffer's fear of being guilty of hypocrisy was a sign of his true humility. As a leader looks at himself in penitence and realises how far he is from the perfection of Christ he may have to echo the words of Paul in Romans 7, 'What a wretched man I am!' Although that may be a necessary realisation for a time, the leader needs to move on to the affirmations of Romans 8, and rejoice that there is 'now no condemnation', that he is one of 'God's children', and that nothing 'will be able to separate us from the love of God that is in Jesus our Lord'. If he does not he will be too conscious of his own humanity and not enough of the grace of God which is working within him and be tortured by self-doubt and self-contempt.

There are however many legitimate benefits which we should accept as part of the loving kindness of God. Nor should we be too mealy mouthed about it. Christian leadership has many compensations. The business world has long since recognised that 'the things that get rewarded get done'. More recently it has also seen that the rewards that matter to people are far more than the wage packet. This is particularly true of middle-management. LeBoeuf summarises current thinking: 'Among such rewards for good work as money . . . time off . . . profit sharing . . . prizes – are recognition . . . advancement . . . freedom . . . personal growth . . . fun.'[7] Full-time Christian ministry does not usually provide much money, but it can supply many of the other 'rewards'. In leading a local church personal creativity can flourish with a good deal of freedom, and a fair share of recognition. Ministry will make use of all our skills, all our personality and all our possibilities. To make the best of one's life for God and to develop one's abilities to help others are not unworthy motives.

It is good that 'fun' is listed as one of the rewards that people look for. Any church will provide an endless source of comedy to anyone with an ounce of humour. A sense of the ridiculous can puncture any stuffy meeting or pompous churchy occasion. But there is more than just the comic. There is the fun of being with God's people, the *frisson* of delight as we recognise the 'finger of God' in the commonplace, and the quieter pleasure of knowing ourselves to be in God's place at the right time. Laughter often seems to be used by God to dissolve hurts, mend relationships, and usher in the gifts of the Spirit. Christian leaders can be too serious, too intense and earnest, and unwittingly portray a Gospel which is so grim that nobody wants to get involved.

Training new leaders

For many leaders the formation of the next generation of leaders is one of the most satisfying parts of ministry. Whether these will mainly minister within one's own church or more widely is unimportant. Just as Christ had a few like Peter, James and John who were to some extent chosen out of the other apostles for special treatment, so Christian leaders will be selecting and training those who seem to have the possibility of leadership within them. Paul wanted the hesitant Timothy to realise that he was an essential link in four generations of leaders: 'the things you have heard me say . . . entrust to reliable men who will also be qualified to teach others'.[8] A healthy organisation should be capable of producing tomorrow's leaders from within, but it requires a leadership which knows how to select and to train.

The best training concentrates on getting the right attitudes rather than just the skills of ministry. As Gerald Williams, the tennis commentator, said, 'The best coaches do not tell you how to play a forehand or a backhand: they tell you what to think.' The best counselling comes not from a deep knowledge of technique but from an attitude of love. The ability to lead people in worship comes from a heart which is itself worshipping, rather than from lessons in elocution or liturgy. This is not to deny the usefulness of expertise, but to underline that the manner in which it is exercised must be paramount. It is not technically difficult to lead a funeral, but the attitude of the leader to the congregation is all-important.

Many church leaders are called upon from time to time to help train someone who comes as curate, supernumerary minister or assistant pastor. This training is by no means only the preserve of the vicar or minister. It is the church which trains him or her and again attitude-training is more important than precise techniques. There is one area in which churches often fail with the result that the newcomer never feels at home and the whole experience is depressing. The process of 'induction' when a person first arrives can be crucial for their own happiness and the good of the church. Too often they are left to discover things for themselves, and find they have tripped over some unwritten custom and offended many. Induction is described as 'the process of helping the newcomer to adjust as quickly as possible to the new social and working environment in order to achieve maximum effectiveness in the shortest possible time'. It means familiarising them with the 'rules, codes, jargon . . . accepted customs and practice'.[9] Good businesses spend a fair amount of trouble on this induction process, for they know that only when a newcomer feels safe and accepted are they going to learn – and become profitable to the company.

Leadership is usually caught rather than taught. Only a limited amount can be learnt from books or lectures. Christ used 'apprenticeship training' for the leaders of the future church, and the gospels are our best guide. The thing which stands out from the most casual glance at his relationship with them is that he was prepared to take great risks. He challenged their basic assumptions, threw apparently unanswerable questions at them, allowed them to operate far from his side. He did not answer all their questions, and left them frequently bewildered and confused. He allowed them to fail humiliatingly and publicly. And he was able to do all this because of one fact – they knew that he loved them *eis telos*, 'to the uttermost'.[10] He showed them his miracles, but also his vulnerability – the scars on 'his hands and his side'. He opened his heart to them and laid down his life for them. He finally departed from them leaving only the promise of his Spirit. He had not given them sermon classes, but they had heard him preach. He had not taught them to lead worship, but he had taught them to pray. And having trained them in this way he sent them to the world.

If this model of training is followed then the undergirding of absolute love and support must be given to the new leader, both by the person who is responsible for training and by the whole church. And part of this will be a personal openness of the teacher and the church to the disciple. We do not know if Christ consciously modelled his training on that of the rabbis, but they kept their disciples around them, ate with them, journeyed with them. The students were meant to copy every gesture and inflexion of voice.[11] Certainly his methods of training were more akin to the rabbinic model than the normal lecture-room pattern of today. One minister was following this model with a young man who was thinking towards ordination. He did not only guide his reading but took every opportunity to take him with him when he was ministering – visiting the sick, instructing couples for marriage, preparing sermons. Wherever possible he gave a running commentary while he was doing it, or debriefed afterwards. Talking to the young man I was conscious that he was not merely learning the techniques of ministry but learning at a deeper level to be a minister. This he was absorbing, not from what he was being told, but from the personality of the older man. He was learning what it was like to spend himself in the service of others, to interweave prayer and action, to be a man of God. The minister on the other hand was all too conscious of the inadequacy of his explanations and the deficiencies in his ministry, though he did say that the presence of the other gave him a greater sharpness and concentration in what he was doing. But this seemed to me to be closer to the training given by Christ to the disciples than the seminary model which is normal in the western world.

This apprenticeship or rabbinic method of training has one great advantage. Although it may appear to take longer and is certainly more demanding of both the teacher and the taught, once something is learnt it remains. The master craftsman guides the hand of the apprentice until he does it right – and that skill will be with him for the rest of his life. Just as it is said we can never forget how to ride a bicycle once it is mastered, an attitude of ministry which is absorbed in this way will never leave us.

After a time there needs to be the right kind of accreditation by the church. If someone is called to be part of a local team leadership then there should be some public occasion in that church when he or she is affirmed. For someone who is called to wider ministry there will be the larger occasion when representatives of the whole church will be present.

But we should not be in too much of a hurry to accredit. I have come across too many teams where 'elders' have been too readily affirmed and then proved to have faults of personality or weaknesses in their spiritual life which show that they were not yet suitable. Possibly we ought to copy the Pentecostal churches of South America which do not ordain pastors until they have passed their apprenticeship and successfully done a series of tasks: 'ordination is thus a seal on effective ministry already undertaken, rather than a mark of transition from academic study to pastoral work, which may or may not prove fruitful'.[12]

The other side of stress

That the ministry of the leader is stressful goes without saying, and in Chapter 8 we looked at the ways stress arises. But there are two aspects of this.

Some stress is seen as negative ('distress'). Feelings of working frantically in an endless dark tunnel, of frustration and of confusion can, if continued, lead to that long-term exhaustion of soul and body which is called 'burnout'.[13] But not all stress is bad. Feelings of personal achievement, the joy of overcoming problems, the bringing of the creative to birth, can all bring positive feelings ('eustress').

In his book *Ministry Burnout*, John Sandford identified nine areas which are of particular difficulty for ministers. It is noticeable that each of these can also be seen as areas of hope:

The job is never finished	BUT THIS MEANS	there are always new stimuli for thought and action
We often cannot see any results		we do not have the tyranny of achieving goals that most have to face
The work is repetitious		we have a framework into which to inject freshness

We always have to deal with the expectations of others	we have an opportunity to be our own person and follow 'God's good, pleasing and perfect will'
We must work a great deal with the same people	we can establish a real fellowship and outpost of the Kingdom
Working with those in need saps our energy	therefore we need to draw on the unlimited power of God
Many come, not for solid spiritual food, but for 'strokes'	we have the opportunity to turn their personal need for love towards Christ
We have to function often behind a mask	it gives an opportunity to be vulnerable, to step off the pedestal and be ourselves
We can become exhausted by failure	that we learn the path of the Christ

It may be over-simplistic to see difficulties in this way, but it is noticeable that effective leaders rejoice in the hurly-burly of church life and ride the waves because they see the opportunities, while others sink because their attitude is basically negative.

Good leaders never stop being disciples. They are always

learning more about the job, picking up every scrap of experience and information which will enable their ministry to be better fulfilled. They are people of prayer and growing holiness and dedication. Above all they know that as servants, shepherds, stewards and *episkopoi* of the Lord they have a calling of extraordinary variety and infinite interest. Whether they preside at the Eucharist or help the poor, whether they explain the Gospel to a crowd of thousands or to a mentally handicapped girl, they are about the work of the Lord. There can be nothing more satisfying than that.

Notes

pages 1–5

Introduction

1. One recent study in an Anglican diocese, which examined those churches which were growing or declining in numbers, showed that the quality of the clergy was crucial. It also found (a) that congregations grew or declined surprisingly quickly (a quarter of the churches had changed by more than 30% in a three-year period) and (b) that growth was most likely in churches which initially had between 40 and 100 members.

2. Mark 10:43. The scriptural teaching on leadership is covered in Chapter 2.

3. The same process of centralisation is taking place in non-episcopal churches. I trust non-Anglicans will translate any words in the book which seem to have a denominational bias.

4. We seem to be returning to a society which does not know Law, and is therefore sharing Paul's experience: 'I would not have known what sin was except through the law': Rom. 7:7.

5. The work of the sociologists G. Ahern and G. Davie, *Inner City God* (1987).

6. D. Francis and M. Woodcock, 'The junior management squeeze', *Management Today* (1975).

7. It is instructive to reread the books by Hal Lindsey and others published in the early 1970s and see how few of their prophecies have come true.

8. The importance of this collection at the time Paul was writing many of his epistles is fascinating: cf. Acts 11:27–30; 1 Cor. 16:1–3; 2 Cor. 8:9–15; Acts 24:17.

9. C. Handy, *Gods of Management* (1985).

10. David Barrett's statistics in *World Christian Encyclopaedia* are remarkable. He suggests that the figures are: 1958: 12m Pentecostals; 1977: 50m Pentecostals and charismatics; 1987: 277m Pentecostals and charismatics and those who do not use either label 'but exhibit such attitudes in prayer and ministry'. The present total, he believes, is 17.5% of all Christians.

11. Prov. 22:13.
12. J. Child, *Organisation: a guide to problems and practices.*
13. In the USA nearly 7000 students had been enrolled in various Doctor of Ministry programmes by 1984: cf. *A Study of Doctor of Ministry Programs,* as conducted by Auburn and Hartford Seminaries, 1987. In the UK such courses as the MA/Diploma at Westminster College, Oxford, the Lincoln Diploma, the 'Changing Church Course' at Birmingham, and the work of the Urban Theology Unit at Sheffield are all noteworthy. There is however still a great need for some British equivalent of the D.Min. for ministers in mid-vocation.
14. Dictionary definitions of 'administration' and 'management' tend to overlap considerably. Generally modern usage sees management as referring to the whole subject and administration as an element within it.
15. J. H. Fichter, *Religion as an Occupation* (1961). J. H. Simpson, *Study of the Role of the Protestant Parish Minister with special reference to Organisation Theory* (1965), says the minister is 'the chief executive of the local congregation who may spend a large amount of time performing specific professional tasks'.
16. In Britain a 'manager' in the modern sense was impossible before the limited liability statutes of 1856 and 1862.
17. Francis and Woodcock, *The Unblocked Manager* (1982).
18. P. F. Drucker, *Innovation and Entrepreneurship* (1985).
19. P. F. Drucker, *Management* (1977).
20. And it is also basically amoral. The words 'functional' and 'dysfunctional', much used in management thinking, betray this non-ethical standpoint. Would slavery still exist in the western world if it could be shown to be 'functional'?
21. P. Rudge, *Ministry and Management* (1968).

Chapter 1. Look at the People

1. It was not always thus. In the early third century (e.g. Hippolytus) it was preparation for baptism that took three years; ordination was a comparatively simple affair. The candidate for baptism went through daily exorcisms, with much time spent in prayer and fasting. The service of baptism was one of the highlights of the year with elaborate symbolic ritual: baptism, anointing with oil, white dress, sharing the kiss of peace, the Eucharist, and milk and honey. Ordination often took a few minutes at a Sunday liturgy.
2. John Tiller (1983).

3. E. E. Jones, *The Management of Ministry* (1978).
4. P. F. Drucker, *Management* (1977).
5. For details of this research see Chapter 6.
6. P. S. Minear, *Images of God in the New Testament* (1960).
7. *Splanchnizomai* is one of the great words of the New Testament, and describes well the attitude a minister should have to those he helps. It is almost untranslatable: 'to have pity' or 'to be filled with compassion' (NIV) are far too weak. It describes the minister's whole being yearning in love for the good of his people: cf. esp. Mark 1:41; 6:34; Luke 7:13; 15:20.
8. 'There is no greater indictment of an organisation than that the strength and ability of the outstanding individual threatens the group and that his or her performance becomes a source of difficulty, frustration and discouragement for others.' Drucker, op cit.
9. This use of the word by management theorists is somewhat different from its use in philosophy where it describes the process of converting an abstract concept into a thing.
10. D. Silverman, *The Theory of Organisations* (1970).
11. The informal structure 'arises from the interaction of people working in the organisation and the development of groups with their own relationships and norms of behaviour, irrespective of those defined within the formal structure. The informal organisation is flexible and loosely structured. Relationships may be left undefined. Membership is spontaneous and with varying degrees of involvement', J. Mullins, *Management and Organisational Behaviour* (1985).
12. R. Blake and J. Mouton, *Advanced Management Office Executive* (1962); a further development of it is in *The New Managerial Grid* (1978). In this they suggest that the style of management in any situation is influenced by (a) the underlying philosophy of the organisation, (b) the nature of the problem, (c) the personal values of the manager, (d) the personality of the manager, and (e) chance, that is, has the manager encountered this sort of situation before?
13. 'When personality tests are given to low-, average- and top-performing managers, top performers show the greatest tendency to take risks. Low-level performers long for security and try to appear important without taking risks. Average performers are less security conscious, but are preoccupied with looking effective rather than being effective. Peak performers . . . enjoy work for its own sake, and care less about security.' M. LeBoeuf, *How to Motivate People* (1986).
14 D. McGregor, *The Human Side of Enterprise* (1960).
15. A. Maslow, *Eupsychian Management*.

16. cf. Gal. 5:23; Acts. 24:25.
17. He has been criticised particularly for what he called the 'prepotency of needs', whereby each level of need has to be met before the satisfaction of higher-order needs has any effect. It may be wiser to see the triangle in the form of a circle with five segments – any one of which may be uppermost at any one time for a particular individual.
18. There is a delicious portrayal of this problem in H. Bashford, *Augustus Carp Esq.: the autobiography of a really good man*.
19. At the Nationwide Initiative in Evangelism Conference, Nottingham, 1980.
20. Quoted in J. Tiller, *A Strategy for the Church's Ministry* (1983).
21. R. Niebuhr, *The Purpose of the Church and its Ministry* (1956).
22. An interesting attempt to link appropriate spiritualities with certain personality types (using the Myers–Briggs classifications) has been made by I. Williams, *Prayer and My Personality* (1987).

Chapter 2. The Nature of Christian Leadership

1. M. Woodcock and D. Francis, *The Unblocked Manager* (1982).
2. Stewart, *The Reality of Management*.
3. This is modified from D. McGregor, *The Professional Manager* (1967).
4. D. Watson, *Discipleship* (1982; US edn. *Called and Committed*), lists 21 scriptural requirements of a leader. Many of them are referred to in the section 'The behaviour of the leader', but of the personality traits which are mentioned nearly all centre around integrity, self-confidence in one's ministry, and wisdom.
5. E. Gibbs, *Followed or Pushed* (1987).
6. The brief sentence of Gal. 3:3, 'after beginning with the Spirit, are you now trying to attain your goal by human effort', could sadly be applied to many Christian ministers.
7. A. Bittlinger, *Gifts and Ministries* (1973).
8. 1 Cor. 3:12.
9. Rom. 12:6–8; 1 Cor. 12:27–31; Eph. 4:11–13; 1 Pet. 4:10f. P. Wagner, *Your Spiritual Gifts* (1979), lists 27 charisms in the New Testament. In Rom. 12:8 the verb *proistemi* is used: 'let the one who rules [or 'presides'] do so eagerly', but, although it is a generalised word for leadership, it appears not to have been used normally.
10. The Society of Friends is an exception to this, as in much else. They have been able to function without an official 'extra-local' dimension for centuries. This may well derive from their rejection

of the sacraments, for any such rite has to be seen as the action of the whole church, with some being excluded and others admitted. This in turn raises questions of legality which cannot be answered for long on a purely local basis. Even in this case there are informal gatherings of those who are regarded as having particular influence in the different churches.

11. Rom. 12:3.
12. 'In appraising themselves people tend to be either too critical or not critical enough. They are likely to see their strengths in the wrong places and pride themselves on non-abilities rather than abilities.' P. F. Drucker, *Management* (1977).
13. For example, Drucker lists 6, Krech 14, while Stewart and Minzberg settle for 3.
14. Mark 10:42.
15. Woodcock and Francis, op. cit.
16. 1 Cor. 9:19; Phil. 2:17.
17. Luke 22:27.
18. 'The Ordering of Priests', Book of Common Prayer.
19. M. LeBoeuf, *How to Motivate People* (1986). Ray Bakke, speaking of his inner city experience, would also wish to spend a fifth of his time on 'networking', that is, making contact with other ministers, social agencies, businesses, police etc. R. Bakke, *The Urban Christian* (1987).
20. LeBoeuf, op. cit.
21. Transference can be defined as the process whereby someone projects on to the counsellor some of the irrational feelings he had towards his parents.
22. This is sometimes seen when the church cries out for more 'leadership'. This may be right but it may be a desire for a dependant position under a more authoritarian style of leadership. Israel's demand for a king in 1 Sam. 8 is very instructive.
23. Especially valuable is K. Leech, *Soul Friend* (1977).
24. The usual word in the New Testament is *oikonomos*; less frequent is *epitrope*, which has virtually the same meaning.
25. Eph. 1:10; 1 Pet. 4:10.
26. J. Bax, *The Good Wine* (1986).
27. Bishop Colin Buchanan has an interesting theory that *kubernesis* refers to someone who leads worship: *Leading Worship* (Grove Books, Worship 76). *Kubernesis* is only used at 1 Cor. 12:28 so it is impossible to be sure, but it is a good description of conducting worship – steering it along, as a helmsman guides a ship or a conductor controls an orchestra.
28. Principally by Bishop Lightfoot in his commentary on Philippians (1868). The main passages in the argument are: Acts 20:28 where

Paul addresses the *presbuteroi* of Ephesus as *episkopoi*; Tit. 1:5 where Titus is told to appoint *presbuteroi* and is then given a list of the requirements for an *episkopos*; and 1 Pet. 5:2 where *presbuteroi* are told to exercise *episkopountes* over the flock.

29. Acts 3:15.

30. A. W. Tozer.

31. J. White and K. Blue, *Healing the Wounded* (1985).

32. Matt. 18:15. The whole of Matthew 18 is important in this context, and not just the well-known vv. 15–20, for it contains teaching about the importance of facing up to sin, the love of God in seeking the sinner and the limitless nature of God's forgiveness.

33. Matt. 18:16; cf. 1 Tim. 5:19.

34. Matt. 18:17; cf. 2 Cor. 5:8. ('reaffirm your love for him'); 1 Tim. 5:20. Only after this should a person be excluded from the fellowship: 1 Cor. 5:1–5,13; 1 Tim. 1:20.

35. Stewart, *Managers and their Jobs.*

36. 'Personal specifications' are increasingly used alongside 'job specifications' when people are sought for a post. This spells out the sort of personality characteristics which the job requires rather than the details of the work entailed. They are particularly important when senior positions are to be filled.

37. The lists distinguish between *presbuteros/episkopos* and *diakonos*: the requirements for the first are given in 1 Tim. 3:1–7; Tit. 1:6–9; 1 Pet. 5:1–4; and for a deacon in 1 Tim. 3:8–13. Other passages which describe something of the work of a leader are Acts 20:18f; 1 Thess. 5:12–14; Heb. 13:7; Jas. 5:14–16.

38. Is emotional freedom a function of latitude – Swedes often see the English as much more open than themselves, while the English regard the Mediterranean peoples as disturbingly ebullient.

39. 2 Cor. 7:4.

40. John 17:19 (AV).

41. Phil. 1:4–6.

Chapter 3. The Team

1. The opposite of the 'flower-pot' church is the 'bottle' church in which the minister is the cork! 'Nothing can go in or out except through him. No meetings can take place unless he is the leader or chairman. No decisions can be made without his counsel or approval. This bottle concept of the church makes growth and maturity virtually impossible. Members are unable to develop into the God-given ministry they could well experience because, in

structure and in practice, there is room for only one minister.' D. Watson, *I Believe in the Church* (1978).

2. Woodcock and Francis, *The Unblocked Manager* (1982).

3. C. Handy, *Gods of Management* (1985).

4. Acts 14:23; Tit. 1:5.

5. And of David Wasdell of the Church Urban Unit: *Divide and Conquer* (1976). More detailed work suggests that the number that can adequately be pastored by one person is about 60; there will be others in the congregation who are not pastored but are content to be members. The number of these additional members is largely dependent on sociological factors. In a UPA it may be a handful, in a suburban church it may be many more. The total figure of 175 which is often quoted has to be understood as being a rough average.

6. J. Tiller, *A Strategy for the Church's Ministry* (1983), ch. 15, examines the possibilities of 'elders' in an Anglican setting.

7. C. Blair, *The Man who could do no Wrong* (1982), asks, 'Are your co-workers a completion of yourself? Or simply an extension? If I am called to leadership and find helpers who are simply echoes of myself, I double my strengths but I also double my weaknesses.'

8. Brian Walker, the director of the major charity, Oxfam, speaking from his experience of dealing with people in his organisation comments, 'Highly motivated people who step aside from the normal pattern of career development, almost by definition are very difficult to 'manage'. Powerful creativity is highly volatile material. Commitment is only one step removed from fanaticism. Dedication can degenerate into dogmatism. Zeal can become zealotry,' quoted in R. Wild, ed., *How to Manage* (1982). He could be speaking of many church leaders.

9. 'If the span of control is too wide it becomes difficult to supervise subordinates effectively and places more stress on the manager . . . if it is too narrow this may present a problem of coordination and consistency in decision-making.' L. Mullins, *Management and Organisational Behaviour* (1985). Peter Drucker wishes to replace the idea of a span of control with a more meaningful concept: 'the span of managerial relationships'. 'It is not how many people have to report to a manager that matters. It is how many people who have to work with each other report to a manager.' In a church context this means being aware of the rapidly growing number of relationships which an increase in the number in a team involves. One can only work closely in a complex organisation like a church with a limited number of people.

10. cf. Administry Project Resource Paper 87:1. This is an excellent

survey of 57 Anglican parishes where team leadership is in operation or has been considered. Many of the practical questions are raised in it.

11. J. Tiller and M. Birchall, *The Gospel Community and its Leadership* (1987).

12. S. Garrett, *Manage your Time* (1985).

13. This is often reflected in financial terms. It has been found that those in UPA congregations give more per head to the work of their church than those in other areas, ACUPA 7.64. The poor give more than the rich, not just in relative but in absolute terms.

14. ACUPA 6.8.

15. This is an early example of the Peter Principle. Peter and Hall, 'In a hierarchy every employee tends to rise to his level of incompetence' in *The Peter Principle* (1970).

16. E. A. Jacques, *A General Theory of Bureaucracy*.

17. A rather impersonal 'preparation form' for this purpose is set out in D. Cormack, *Team Spirit* (1987), pp. 177–9.

Chapter 4. The Skeleton

1. Exod. 18:21.

2. It is salutary to remember that Peter Rudge himself said, 'Sociological inquiry has shown that, irrespective of source or doctrine, many churches have in fact assumed a common organisational character', *Ministry and Management* (1968).

3. C. Handy, *Gods of Management*, (2nd edn 1985): Zeus represents entrepreneural leadership, working through loyalty; Apollo is hierarchical and predictable; Athena works through interlocking task groups; while followers of Dionysius are independent professionals.

4. Basically representing the traditional and classical patterns respectively (in Rudge's terminology).

5. Drucker, *Management* (1977).

6. Mullins, *Management and Organisational Behaviour* (1985).

7. Rudge, op. cit.

8. cf. Henry David Thoreau: 'It is not enough to be busy . . . the question is "What are we busy about?" '

9. D. Sheane, *Beyond Bureaucracy* (1976).

10. It is interesting that sports teams vary in number from about 4 to 15, with 11 being common. Does this represent the largest number of people who can work together in that particular environment? Imagine a basketball team of 15 or a Rugby team of 40. The

most effective groups tend to be about 8 and the most effective committees about 10 in number.

11. There are also those who would say it is essentially middle-class and inappropriate in a UPA. To be effective on a committee demands verbal dexterity, the ability to anticipate others, an awareness of the dynamics of a group and self-confidence. These are seldom gifts readily found in inner-city areas.

12. There are different titles for a working party. Laurie Mullins (op. cit.) calls them 'Project Teams': they need 'a clear objective, a well-defined task, a definite end result to be achieved, and a carefully chosen team of people'.

13. This was put most trenchantly by Lyndall Urwick: 'Every organisation and every part of the organisation must be an expression of the purpose of the undertaking concerned, or it is meaningless and therefore redundant.'

14. The aim of the parochial church council in the Synodical Government Measure is useful, and can be adapted for other denominations: 'To cooperate with the incumbent in promoting in the parish the whole mission of the Church, pastoral, evangelistic, social and ecumenical' (SGM 6.2.2).

15. One businessman said to me about a church committee: 'This is the only meeting where I can speak my mind and not need to watch my back.'

16. Authors use different terms: 'line' and 'support' were coined by Mintzberg, while Joan Woodward uses 'task' and 'element'.

17. J. Child, *Organisations: a guide to problems and practice*.

18. The term was invented by the French economist J.-B Say about 1800. The former head of British Rail, Sir Peter Parker, reckoned 'one entrepreneur can recognise another at 300 yards on a misty day. This is an area of imagination and energy, of risk-taking and risk-making, of seizing chances that others do not seize, of seeing ahead and somehow letting the future have your ways.' That is a fair description of St Paul. The church must allow for such people.

19. Useful books on committee procedure are legion: particularly useful are W. Fletcher, *Meetings, Meetings* (1985); M. Beech, *How to make Meetings Work* (1983); and G. Wainwright, *Meetings and Committee Procedure* (1987).

20. Peter Drucker cites the case of a chemical company which was about to discontinue a standard machine. They informed their customers, who ordered additional spare parts. The clerk in the stores department, who had not been told of the decision, responded to the spurt in sales, and, following instructions, ordered material sufficient for another 8 years.

Chapter 5. Where is the Church?

1. *Mission Audit* (1985) published by the Board of Mission and Unity. The phrase and the ideas behind it are used in many denominations. (In ACUPA the phrase 'parish audit' is used.)
2. The word 'convict' in John 16:8 has this meaning. The Holy Spirit does not just inform the world of the facts about sin, righteousness and judgement, he portrays spiritual realities so that they can elicit true responses from people: guilt, wonder, awe, etc. It is probably best translated 'expose to the light'; the Greek does not have the harshness of the English word 'convict'.
3. Since assessment is often used by management as a disciplinary control, these are sometimes called 'control systems'. However an audit in the church should only be used in this way in the case of major breakdown, and the term is therefore misleading.
4. Church Growth has also been heavily criticised for its statement of the 'homogeneous principle': that church growth is most rapid within a community of people from the same culture and background. As a statement of fact it cannot be faulted; it is only when some of its proponents go on to suggest that churches should therefore not engage in cross-cultural evangelism that it seems to contradict the universality of the Gospel.
5. 1 Cor. 9:26.
6. So when Drucker says 'management by objectives and self-control makes the interest of the enterprise the aim of every manager' he betrays some naïvety about the way human groups operate.
7. Phil. 3:12–14.
8. Etzioni, *Modern Organisations* (1964).
9. There are two thought-provoking Greek words in this verse: *sunschematizesthe* refers to a coin being made by pressing a soft metal such as gold into a mould; *metamorphousthe* comes from the word for transfiguration. Hence Paul sees the Christian as one who attempts to be free from pressures (educational, commercial, racial) to think in a culturally-conditioned manner, and to have a metamorphosis of his or her whole way of thinking.
10. Particularly useful are *Mission Pursuit* published by the United Reformed Church (86 Tavistock Place, London); and systems for audit set up by certain Anglican dioceses under such titles as *Parish Development, Mission Audit, Planning for Growth* etc. The pack produced by the Milton Keynes ecumenical team deserves a special mention.
11. I have used the plural in talking about consultants because, in my experience, two heads are better than one in this field. The team of two or more may give each other support, widen the perspective

when assessing the church, bring different skills, and lend greater weight to their eventual report. It is useful if there is both lay and clerical representation in the team, for they tend to look at ecclesiastical matters differently, and the lay person is often a better judge of the wider community.

12. There are two kinds of 'encouragement': 'negative reinforcement' which punishes mistakes, and 'positive reinforcement' which praises work and raises people's status.

13. The Greek word *gonguzo* onomatopaeically describes the grumbling which is so destructive in a church, and so roundly condemned in the Bible: 1 Cor. 10:10: John 6:41 etc.

14. The figures were gathered between 1984 and 1987 in Nottinghamshire. Statistics gathered by Gavin Reid in the late 1970s yield very similar results: 'Exorcising Evangelism', *Mission and Unity Digest* (BMU, 1987). The figures should not, of course, be taken as universally applicable. Each church needs to produce its own.

15. Frendle and Raven distinguish different kinds of power: reward power: ability to give people what they want; coercive power: ability to make people obey; legitimate power: respect for lawful authority; referrent power: respect for an individual, hero-worship; expert power: special knowledge or skill. Church leaders need to assess what kinds of power they exercise. It is not difficult to produce a diagram showing the dynamics of power in an organisation and where they collide or collude with each other.

16. D. Pytches, *Come, Holy Spirit* (1985).

17. Woodcock and Francis, op. cit.

18. This is usually seen in the form of a Gantt Chart which sets out the stages through which a project has to go before completion. By allocating the time needed for each stage it is possible to discover the shortest time in which the enterprise can be finished and those stages which are of critical importance. It is of value for church leaders in planning some major project or event.

19. Matt. 6:33.

Chapter 6. Changing Things

1. Ministers sometimes seek to bypass these structures which can appear cumbersome. But the responsibility for a decision is no longer shared, and since he has not involved others in it, they will leave him to carry it out and he will become a 'paid servant' of the congregation. If he does not look for help, he will not receive it.

2. 'Management is making things happen and this means causing change. If you have not decided what you want to make happen, if what you want is unrealistic because it does not relate to the world as it is or will be, if it requires resources which you do not have or cannot create, if you do not make your plans known to those who have to carry them out, you have not started.' C. T. Wyatt, chairman of the Costain Group.

3. Quoted in Administry paper 87.6.

4. *Tales of a Traveller* (1824).

5. Most of the Israelites could not cope with the vision of conquering the Promised Land. As a result they suffered a catastrophic decline in their perception of self-worth and the ability of God to help: 'we seemed like grasshoppers in our own eyes . . . why is the Lord bringing us to this land only to let us fall by the sword?' (Num. 13:33 and 14:3).

6. It is often assumed that ministers are by nature and training innovators. In fact Peter Wagner, *Leading your Church to Growth* (1986), suggests 'Research concludes that 5% of American pastors *invent*. They are creative and can design their own programmes. Another 15% *adapt*. They are innovative and have the ability to take principles and programmes that someone else comes up with and tailor them to fit their particular situation. But then a full 80% of pastors *adopt*. They are not particularly interested in making up their own programmes or introducing changes in an existing programme.'

7. This can sometimes be avoided by having the suggestion made from outside the local church. It was found in an Anglican diocese that a far higher proportion of parishes adopted a mission audit package when it was put to the PCC by a diocesan adviser rather than their own incumbent. This was because the latter was able to be more relaxed, see how people were reacting to the idea, and not demand commitment to it too soon.

8. Administry paper 87.6.

9. 3 John 9,10.

10. People outside the congregation may need to be consulted. One church that lacked anyone between the ages of 20 and 40 approached non-churchgoers in that age range and asked for their reactions. Major changes were initiated because of their response.

11. Many churches have found that the use of a questionnaire for discovering congregational opinion needs care. This method is easy and gives everyone an opportunity to express their views, but it can harden attitudes and polarise opinion unnecessarily if it is done too late in the decision-making process.

12. 'Any inhabitant of an organisation will have perceived the law of

the pendulum at work as the organisation centralises, then a few years later decentralises, only to centralise again in due course. Here the organisation is intuitively searching for a new balance; it swings from central information to a mixture of groups and liaison and back again. The search for balance is never ending.' Woodcock and Francis, op. cit.

Chapter 7. The Effects of Spiritual Renewal

1. The *cursillo* movement originated in Spain, moved to South America, and from there entered the USA. In recent years it has become fairly widespread in Anglican and Roman Catholic churches in Europe. It is based on a single, never-to-be-repeated three-day conference, followed by the 'Fourth Day': a lifetime of commitment and fellowship.
2. 1 Cor. 14:40.
3. Luke 11:1.
4. It is instructive that Paul described partisanship within a church as *'hairesis'*, which can also be translated 'sect' or even 'heresy': cf. Acts 24:5; 26:5; 28:22; 1 Cor. 11:19; Gal. 5:20; 2 Pet. 2:1.
5. 1 Cor. 3:10.
6. This love is very different from the 'love-bombing' of the Moony and other cults. Theirs is a cloying love with an ulterior motive, to encourage people to suspend their judgement and join the sect.
7. As Cardinal Suenens, a leader of the charismatic renewal in the Roman Catholic Church, says, 'Charisphobia is caused by charismania'.
8. John Finney and F. Lawson, *Saints Alive!* (1983) pub. by Anglican Renewal Ministries.
9. The title of a book by Barry Kissell.
10. The parish of Tollerton where I served has records of the fierce opposition to the introduction of the organ in 1868, which ousted the six-piece orchestra.
11. Any exception to this is when the UPA church is made up of people from the suburbs who commute to their old church; these will be very resistant to any alteration in what for some is the family shrine.
12. Deut. 32:15 ('Jeshurun' is descriptive of Israel – 'the upright one').
13. Exod. 34:15.
14. Deut. 9:6.
15. John 3:30.

Chapter 8. The Strains of Leadership

1. Cromwell's words written to a friend who was taking a stand on 'principle', still bear repetition: 'I beseech you, in the bowels of Christ, to believe that you may be mistaken.'
2. Gal. 2:11.
3. cf. Phil. 4:5; 1 Tim. 3:3 (where it is a desiderata for elders).
4. This section is heavily dependent upon Robert Blake and Jane Mouton, *Managing Intergroup Conflict* (1964).
5. Mark 10:35–45.
6. Mark 7:21–23.
7. Ps. 55:6.
8. 'Supervisors can help themselves by systematically analysing the pressures they are under and each of the conflicts they have. In our experience this is best undertaken by a discussion group of supervisors from the same organisation.' Woodcock and Francis, op. cit.
9. Handy, *Gods of Management* (1985).
10. A recent survey in Britain showed that ordained ministers work 57 hours a week; bishops worked 72.
11. (1986) See also his earlier work, *The Other Side of '84* (1983) and the more rumbustious work of A Walker, *Enemy Territory* (1987).

Chapter 9. The Joys of Ministry

1. Many businesspeople, conscious of having reached their 'ceiling', are taking early retirement at 50 or so and starting new enterprises. Research has shown that the success rate of such innovations is startlingly high.
2. The report was prepared for the Archbishop's Commission on Urban Priority Areas in 1986. It also showed that there was greater job satisfaction among Evangelical clergy.
3. H.A. Barrington, *Learning about Management* (1984).
4. Verses and allusions in this paragraph come from Luke 11:43; 12:1; 18:9; Matt. 23:5.
5. From her St Colm's lecture given in Edinburgh, 1986.
6. D. Bonhoeffer, *Letters and Papers from Prison*.
7. M. Leboeuf, *How to Motivate People* (1986).
8. 2 Tim. 2:2.
9. G. Garrett, *Manage your Time* (1985). The importance of induction is not confined to stipendiary staff. It also applies to laypeople transferring from another church: one lady who joined a fairly large church spoke of having hardly found her feet after

more than a year of attendance at Sunday worship and midweek meetings.

10. John 13:1.
11. The rabbis would probably not have been too pleased to be informed of it, but they were in fact copying the pattern of the Greek philosophers. Seneca (AD 4–65) said to prospective disciples, 'choose a master whose life, conversation and soul-expressing face have satisfied you: picture him always to yourself as your protector and pattern'. This applied to details: it was said that all Plato's disciples stooped as he did; cf. M. Griffiths, *The Example of Jesus* (1985).
12. T. Beeson and J. Pearch, *Vision of Hope* (1982).
13. Christina Maslach describes 'burnout' as 'a state of physical, emotional and mental exhaustion marked by physical depletion and chronic fatigue, feelings of helplessness and hopelessness, and by the development of a negative self-concept and negative attitudes towards your work, life and other people'.

Bibliography

The literature on management studies is immense, and those who are unfamiliar with management studies might well begin with P. F. Drucker. The number of books of Christian leadership is much more limited, while those that consider such leadership in the light of management studies are few indeed. The following are the books which have been found useful and which are reasonably accessible on both sides of the Atlantic.

G. Ahern and G. Davie, *Inner City God* (Hodders 1987)

R. S. Anderson, ed., *Theological Foundations for Ministry* (Eerdmans 1979)

J. Anderson and E. E. Jones, *The Management of Ministry* (Harper & Row 1978)

M. Archer, *Call Yourself a Manager?* (Mercury 1987)

R. Bakke, *The Urban Christian* (Marc Europe 1987)

H. A. Barrington, *Learning about Management* (McGraw-Hill 1984)

J. Bax, *The Good Wine* (CIO 1986)

Board of Mission and Unity, *Mission Audit* (BMU 1984)

E. de Bono, *Lateral Thinking for Management* (Pelican 1982)

D. Cormack, *Seconds Away* (Mark Europe 1987)

——, *Team Spirit* (Mark Europe 1986)

E. Dayton and E. Engstrom, *Strategy for Leadership* (Mark Europe 1985)

V. J. Donovan, *Christianity Rediscovered* (SCM 1982)

P. F. Drucker, *Management* (Pan Business 1977)

——, *Innovation and Entrepreneurship* (Heinemann 1985)

J. Eddison, *Understanding Christian Leadership* (Scripture Union 1974)

S. Garrett, *Manage your Time* (Fontana 1985)

E. Gibbs, *I believe in Church Growth* (Marc Europe 1987)

——, *Followed or Pushed* (Hodders 1984)

P. Greenslade, *Leadership* (Marshalls 1984)

J. Gunstone, *A People for His Praise* (Hodders 1978)

C. Handy, *Gods of Management* (Pan Business 1985)

J. C. Harris, *Stress, Power and Ministry* (Alban Institute 1977)

P. Lawrence and R. Lee, *Insight into Management* (OUP 1984)

M. LeBoeuf, *How to Motivate People* (Sidgwick & Jackson 1986)

K. Leech, *Soul Friend* (Sheldon 1977)

R. F. Lovelace, *Dynamics of Spiritual Life* (IVP 1979)

P. King, *Leadership Explosion* (Hodders 1987)

J. L. Massie, *Essentials of Management* (Prentice-Hall 1979)

L. J. Mullins, *Management and Organisational Behaviour* (Pitman 1985)

R. Oldcorn, *Management: a Fresh Approach* (Pan Business 1988)

B. Pearson, *Yes, Manager* (Grove Books 1986)

Archbishops' Commission on Urban Priority Areas, *Faith in the City* (CIO 1985)

B. Reed, *The Dynamics of Religion* (DLT 1979)

L. Richards, and C. Hoeldtke, *A Theology of Church Leadership* (Zondervan 1980)

P. F. Rudge, *Ministry and Management* (Tavistock 1968)

L. E. Schaller, *Survival Tactics in the Parish* (Abingdon 1977)

H. A. Snyder, *The Problem of Wineskins* (IVP 1977)

——, *The Community of the King* (IVCF 1976)

J. Tiller, *A Strategy for the Church's Ministry* (CIO 1983)

——, and M. Birchall, *The Gospel Community* (Marshalls 1987)

P. Wagner, *Leading your Church to Growth* (Marc Europe 1984)

M. Woodcock and D. Francis, *The Unblocked Manager* (Gower 1982)

Many of the occasional papers published by Administry are relevant to the subject of this book.